I0815783

# A TASTE OF HONG KONG

## 70 ESSENTIAL RECIPES FROM ASIA'S WORLD CITY

PRESTEL
MUNICH • LONDON • NEW YORK

ADA DESCHANEL & DAVINA CHANG

# CONTENTS

# Hong Kong: A City of Contrasts

Hong Kong is a place where ancient meets modern, East meets West, and nature meets skyscrapers. From its humble beginnings as a fishing village to its present status as a global financial center, Hong Kong has always been a city on the move, shaped by its unique history and diverse influences.

At the heart of this constantly evolving metropolis, Hong Kong's profuse culinary culture is a reflection of its people: dynamic, adaptable, and deeply rooted in tradition. Built on foundations formed by hundreds of years of Cantonese culinary traditions, its flavors have been enriched by British colonial influences, international trade, and waves of immigration. The result is a unique gastronomic landscape where teahouses serving *dim sum*[1] coexist with *dai pai dongs*[2] and Michelin-star restaurants to offer an endless range of flavors and experiences.

Eating in Hong Kong is much more than satisfying a simple daily requirement–it is truly a way of life. Whether it's the comforting warmth of a bowl of wonton soup,[3] the delicate craftsmanship that goes into making freshly steamed *har gow*[4] dumplings, or the simple pleasure of a buttery pineapple bun,[5] each dish tells a story from the city's past and present. The bustling markets, along with the *dai pai dongs* and *cha chaan tengs*,[6] embody the city's fast-paced, characterful, and resolutely authentic spirit.

This book isn't just a collection of recipes. It also delves into Hong Kong's rich culinary heritage and pays tribute to the flavors, techniques, and traditions that make its cuisine unique. Through these pages, we hope to share with you a taste of Hong Kong that will enable you to capture its essence in the meals you prepare, no matter where you are in the world.

---

1. Small pieces of steamed dumplings and other appetizers.
2. Open-air food stalls.
3. Clear soup with pork and/or shrimp dumplings.
4. Steamed shrimp dumplings.
5. See page 20.
6. Food stalls and Hong Kong-style diners.

## DAVINA

I was born and raised in Hong Kong, but for a long time I hesitated to call myself a Hong Konger. Like many of my classmates in the bubble of our international school, I was fascinated by the idea of being a "banana"—yellow on the outside and white on the inside. English flowed from my lips more easily than Cantonese, and I never listened to local music. Although I'd been raised in the rituals of a Cantonese household, my mind followed another set of rules, the ones I'd learned from Hollywood movies.

I left Hong Kong to go to New York in 2012 to spend four years at college. While I was expecting to fit in perfectly, it didn't work out that way. I didn't really feel a culture shock—at least not exactly—but I had an emptiness that I couldn't identify. I began to crave the dishes that were once part of my daily life: the egg tarts, pineapple buns, my mother's sweet-and-sour pork. Chinatown became my second home, a place where I could soothe my homesickness with wontons and congee[7] as I listened to the chatter in Cantonese all around me.

My next move was to Singapore, where, on the surface, I was closer to Hong Kong—at least culturally. But instead of finding answers to my questions, I was feeling more lost than ever. I no longer knew where I belonged, or what I was in terms of identity. Surprisingly, it wasn't until I arrived in Paris in 2019 that I started to feel at home. Despite Hong Kong being so far away, this city instilled in me a sense of belonging, and I feel like I fit in. Regardless, throughout this process, my Hong Kong identity has become stronger and more defined than ever.

Two years ago, I opened Bing Sutt in Paris with the aim of sharing Hong Kong's food culture. The food of Hong Kong is so much more than a simple part of Chinese cuisine; it has its own identity that has been shaped by centuries of migration, colonial influence, and an indefatigable spirit of adaptation. Growing up, I never questioned the fact that we had our own versions of milk tea, spaghetti Bolognese, and even borsch. While seemingly foreign, these dishes are deeply rooted in the city's DNA. At the coffee shop, I never tire of explaining to curious customers why there's no pineapple in the pineapple buns, because every conversation is an opportunity to share a piece of home.

I am grateful to all my customers, whether travelers who have visited Hong Kong or Hong Kongers who have lived here for years. When they talk about their favorite neighborhoods and memories, I see pieces of my own story being reflected in theirs. Their nostalgia reminds me that these memories also belong to me, too. Hong Kong is not only where I come from, but a place that I'm also proud to call "home."

One of the customers who has had the biggest impact on me is Ada, who is also my coauthor. I clearly remember when I first met her. It was a chaotic day, we were having problems in the kitchen, and I couldn't

7. A rice porridge.

bring her the pineapple bun she had ordered. Even so, we managed to start a conversation. From the beginning, it was obvious that she loved Hong Kong. I remember feeling something unexpected—perhaps admiration, even a touch of envy—at the fact that she saw so much beauty in the city that I had always taken for granted.

One day, Ada made me an astonishing proposal. It was a creative project that would combine her passion for Hong Kong with my heritage. However, she was also offering me something far greater—a chance to reconnect with my roots.

That is how this book emerged and would become a step toward reconciling my identity. On my last visit to Hong Kong, I wandered the streets with Ada in search of street food and local specialties. It was then that something awoke inside me. My previous visits had been devoted to discovering new restaurants, often overlooking the nostalgic comfort of Hong Kong cuisine. But during those five days with her, I went back to basics—Tai O doughnuts, Hong Kong-style French toast, red bean ice, and wontons, to name a few. Each bite awakened a memory, taking me back to times shared with family and friends, and reminding me of the flavors that have shaped who I am. I hope that the recipes and texts in this book will offer you a glimpse of the Hong Kong that molded me and let you feel the spirit of that city, of "my home."

## ADA

This book isn't about cooking, or even about the recipes it contains.

It's a love story in which a young Ada is smitten by a city thousands of miles away from her home. It's a city so removed from what she knows that she doesn't want to leave, where she wants to discover, explore, probe, taste, understand, explore, and delve deeper.

It's a story of encounters, filled with smells, tastes, and colors; with men and women; with rattling taxicabs and minibuses with leather seats that stick to your skin in summer; with the rich, sweet taste of milk tea drunk early in the morning at a *chaan teng*; with the sun beating down hard on our foreheads while riding on the back deck of the Star Ferry.

It's a story about discovering a city, its inhabitants, and its neighborhoods: Sheung Wan and Sai Ying Pun, which smell of dried fish, and Happy Valley, with its horses standing guard in front of the mountain. It's about pineapple buns without a trace of pineapple, and glazed meats with sweet and spicy smells.

It's a fantasy that blends waterfalls lost in the mountains with little dumplings encasing wonders, golden egg tarts, and a pirate's cave overlooking crystalline waters.

It's a story about history, travels, traditions, and migrations; about the past meeting the present, acknowledging each other, and coming together in cups and plates and bowls; a story that is told at the metal table of a street hawker restaurant or at the foot of a flight of steps.

It's a story about typhoons that give their name to a crab dish, about the winds and rains that punctuate the rhythm of an unstoppable city, about the sun that dries egg yolks in Tai O and tangerine peels in Cheung Chau.

This is the story of Hong Kong, my soul mate, my friend, my refuge, as seen through my and Davina's eyes.

I'd give anything to wake up every morning in my little apartment on Po Yan Street and go down into the street for tea and scrambled eggs on white toast, sharing a table with strangers. But for all the mornings that I can't—because I'm not there—and for all the afternoons that I can't warm up with a *char siu bao* or cool down with a mango pudding; and for all the evenings that I can't go out for truly hot, soft, and crispy cubes of deep-fried fresh tofu, that I'm unable to wander around under the blinding neon signs of Mong Kok with a red bean ice in my hand, for all those times is why I wanted to write this book and bring together the food that makes Hong Kong what it is. I also wrote it for anybody who misses Hong Kong a little every day, and for foreigners, natives, the curious, the intrigued, former residents of the "fragrant harbor," and everybody else. It's also for my mother, grandmother, brothers, sister, and friends that I wanted to tell stories, this story, and to show them the many fascinating aspects of the city.

Meeting Davina and working together with her has been an experience as rich and smooth as condensed milk, from developing the brief to cowriting the recipes, including our photography shoots in Hong Kong and Paris.

I have found in Davina not only an amazing colleague, but someone with whom I can share my passion back in France and, above all, a friend. Working together has been beneficial, fun, and rewarding. It was amazing to walk with her through the streets of Hong Kong and set up together for a photograph of a dessert on a ladder street or for a shot of a dish in front of a hoarding. I loved the experience of crossing parks while trying to avoid pigeons, being stared at by curious on lookers as I scattered my dishes over the middle of a staircase at Central. Sharing these moments and my vision with Davina was an incredible opportunity.

As I write these lines, I still have little idea of what the baby we are creating will look like. All I know is the heartfelt effort that Davina and I have put into our work, the determination and excitement that has filled us throughout the process, and our eagerness to see it completed and for you to savor it.

## THE HISTORY OF HONG KONG

Hong Kong started out as a small fishing village with just a few thousand inhabitants, but it was strategically located on the Pearl River estuary. Its natural harbor offers protection from the elements, making it an ideal base for maritime trade. In 1842, after the First Opium War, Hong Kong was ceded to Great Britain under the Treaty of Nanjing, marking the onset of more than 150 years of British colonial rule. The city grew into a thriving port during this period, connecting the East with the West by trade and cultural exchange.

Hong Kong's food scene also developed under British rule. The colonial presence introduced Western culinary practices and ingredients, which were fused with traditional Cantonese flavors. Hong Kong became a veritable melting pot of flavors and ideas, where dim sum and barbecued meats were served alongside cream pies and scones, and the custom of afternoon tea would become an essential part of local life in the form of milk tea and egg tarts.

After the handover of Hong Kong to China in 1997, the city entered a new era while retaining its identity. Despite political changes, Hong Kong's culinary culture remains a unique blend of local Cantonese, other Chinese, and international influences. The city continues to be a hub of innovation, with chefs experimenting with creative new ways of using traditional ingredients.

## THE DIFFERENT REGIONS

Whenever I travel to Hong Kong, I am often asked, "So, how's Japan going?" I think Japan is doing well, but I've never been there.

Hong Kong is a special administrative region[8] of the People's Republic of China. It is located on the south coast, adjoining Shenzhen and Guangzhou at the mouth of the Pearl River. Lying halfway between Vietnam to the west and Taiwan to the east, this mountainous and green region covers an archipelago of more than two hundred islands and islets.

## HONG KONG ISLAND

This is the region's second largest island, after Lantau. The north coast, between Kennedy Town in the west and Siu Sai Wan in the east, is the most built-up part.

In the northwest, the lively neighborhoods of Kennedy Town, Sai Ying Pun, and Sheung Wan are popular with young working people and feature many restaurants, bars, independent boutiques, and artists' studios.

8. Political divisions of the country with a high degree of autonomy.

Central is the nerve center of the island and is filled with office towers, shopping malls, luxury boutiques, and banks. This central business district extends westward to Admiralty. After that comes Wan Chai, a diverse district with a bright side and a dark side, filled with shopping areas, coffee shops, and lively places to party to excess.

Causeway Bay is a huge shopping district, but it's also where people go for a quick bite to eat, and there are plenty of food stalls selling sweet and savory snacks. If you head inland from Causeway Bay, you'll soon come across Happy Valley and its iconic racecourse. Farther afield, North Point offers what is considered the Chinatown of the island. This district has far fewer foreign residents, much like Sai Wan Ho, Shau Kei Wan, and Siu Sai Wan.

The south of the island is lined with luxury neighborhoods that have magnificent beaches, such as Repulse Bay, Deep Water Bay, and Stanley. The north and south of the island are separated by a rugged expanse filled with green spaces, such as Tai Tam Country Park, Aberdeen Country Park, and Pok Fu Lam Country Park. In this part of the island, you will also find the Peak, a hill offering a superb panorama of the island and its surroundings.

Hong Kong Island is like a local version of Manhattan, with residents having a reputation for not leaving, and for whom Kowloon is the equivalent of Brooklyn.

## KOWLOON

The area of Kowloon is located on the mainland, across from the island. You can get there by subway, bus, or ferry in the blink of an eye, just like crossing from the Right Bank to the Left Bank in Paris.

Originally a tiny Chinese enclave inside the British colony of Hong Kong, Kowloon Walled City had been dominated by the Triad gangs[9] for many years until it was demolished in 1993.

Today, Kowloon is much more than the remains of a fort the size of four soccer fields. The Kowloon City District is renowned for its night markets (Temple Street), foodie haunts (Sham Shui Po offers the best food experience), and flower and animal markets (Mong Kok). It is also brimming with stores selling kitchenware, opposite the covered market where you can find Hong Kong's finest fruit (also in Mong Kok), and it is where ICC, the city's tallest tower, is located. At the top is the Sky100 observation deck, where you can go for a drink.

Kowloon is the place to go for a more "authentic" local experience, with fewer foreign residents and more Chinese.

---

9. Chinese criminal organizations.

## THE NEW TERRITORIES

The New Territories may be Hong Kong's least visited district, but it accounts for no less than 90 percent of its land area. This is the name given to the stretch of land that separates Kowloon from mainland China. Far from the usual images of skyscrapers and concrete-paved alleyways, the New Territories are a collection of newer neighborhoods, modern towns, and older villages. It is quieter and much less hectic than the rest of the region, and where buildings are no more than three stories high and older people live more by the sun than by the dollar.

You can stroll through Sai Kung, for example, and feel like you're in Thailand, with its long beaches of white sand and crystal-clear water; wander through the Tai Mo Shan Country Park and bathe in the Ng Tung Chai Waterfalls; stroll through the village of Tai Po; or enjoy *yum cha* (see page 82) at a teahouse in Yuen Long. There is so much to do.

## THE OUTLYING ISLANDS

The many islands that surround Hong Kong are a part of the New Territories. They are increasingly popular and offer a quiet (and easily accessible) alternative to the frenetic pace of the urban areas. However, some of the islands, such as Peng Chau and Cheung Chau, do fill up with local tourists in search of tranquility, caves, and beaches. Lantau, the island where both the airport and the Big Buddha are located, is also home to Tai O, a traditional fishing village, and Mui Wo, which is a little less conventional. Lamma is where young families settle down to raise their children in a setting that is more serene than the rest of the region and where a community spirit reigns.

Other, more isolated, outlying islands are only accessible by boat from Sai Kung (unless you charter a private boat from Central Pier) and offer a complete change of scenery, such as Grass Island, which is famous for its wild cattle.

To say that there is a lot to see and discover in Hong Kong is an understatement. Despite visiting regularly for the past seven years, there still so much I haven't seen.

KITAMI
TOKORO·HOKKAIDO
NW 20KG
HOKKAIDO
SIZE

# ESSENTIAL INGREDIENTS

## IN THE HONG KONG KITCHEN

**LIGHT SOY SAUCE (生抽):** This light and salty fermented sauce is used every day to season dishes, whether in marinades, stir-fries, or soups.

**DARK SOY SAUCE (老抽):** A thicker and slightly sweet sauce, it is mainly used to give a richer brown color to meats and stews while it enhances their flavors.

**OYSTER SAUCE (蠔油):** Made from oyster extract, this creamy, umami-rich sauce is ideal for stir-fried vegetables, meats, and, in particular, noodle dishes.

**HOISIN SAUCE (海鮮醬):** A thick and sweet sauce with a hint of spice, it is often used for glazed meats, marinades, and as an accompaniment for crispy aromatic duck.

**CHU HOU SAUCE (柱侯醬):** Made from fermented soybeans, garlic, and spices, this thick, salty-sweet cooking sauce is used for braising meats and in broths and marinades.

**SHA CHA SAUCE (沙茶醬):** A slightly spicy sauce, also known as barbecue sauce or Chinese satay sauce, it is made with soybean oil, garlic, shallots, fish, and dried shrimp. It is used for marinating and enhancing the flavor of other sauces.

**BLACK VINEGAR (黑醋):** The product of a long fermentation process, this mild vinegar has slightly sweet and tangy notes, which are perfect for balancing braised dishes and enhancing sauces.

**RICE VINEGAR (米醋):** This mild and light vinegar is often used in marinades and sauces, and to balance flavors in stir-fried dishes and soups. It adds a hint of freshness without the strong acidity of conventional vinegars.

**SHAOXING WINE (紹興酒):** A slightly sweet and alcoholic wine made from fermented rice that is essential for marinating meats and adding depth to stews and sauces.

**SESAME OIL (芝麻油):** Extracted from toasted sesame seeds, this oil is used as a seasoning after cooking to add a subtle but intense aroma.

**SUN-DRIED SALTED EGG YOLKS (鹹蛋黃):** These are made by preserving duck eggs in salt, which gives them a gritty texture and an umami-rich taste.

**SHRIMP PASTE (蝦醬):** This highly salted and fermented paste adds umami depth to stir-fries and stews, but its intense flavor means that it should be used sparingly.

**DRIED SHRIMP (蝦米):** They may be small, but these shrimp pack a punch with their concentrated seafood flavor when used in stir-fried dishes or added to soups.

**DRIED SHIITAKE MUSHROOMS (冬菇):** The deep, woody flavor of these mushrooms intensifies after rehydration, making them an essential ingredient for broths and stews.

**GINGER (薑):** Pungent and slightly lemony, fresh ginger is used both to marinate meats and flavor soups and stir-fried dishes.

**SCALLIONS (青蔥):** Crunchy when raw and melting in the mouth when cooked, scallions (spring onions) are used in practically all Hong Kong dishes, adding a hint of slightly spicy sweetness.

**GARLIC (蒜頭):** An essential ingredient, it is sautéed, crushed, or minced (very finely chopped) to add a rich flavor and aroma to noodle, meat, and vegetable dishes.

**GROUND WHITE PEPPER (白胡椒粉):** Milder than black pepper, white pepper has a gentle, slightly musky flavor; it is often used to season soups and marinades.

**ROCK SUGAR (冰糖):** A sugar in the form of crystallized lumps, it melts slowly and adds a slight caramelized note to sweeten broths and braised dishes when used in Chinese cooking.

**GLUTINOUS RICE FLOUR (糯米粉):** Also known as sweet rice flour, this is a flour made from glutinous (sticky) rice that is lighter than wheat and gives baked goods (sweet or savory) a sticky and chewy texture.

7 AM / 9 AM →

BREAKFAST
早餐

# THE "FRAGRANT HARBOR"

## *DAVINA*

I took certain things for granted while I was growing up in Hong Kong. Maybe it was because I wasn't particularly curious as a child, but I never wondered why we used chopsticks, or why Hong Kong was called Hong Kong. This knowledge was instinctive, like learning to walk; it was ingrained in me from my earliest years. One day, however, while deep in thought, I had a revelation: Hong Kong literally means "fragrant harbor." Amazed that anyone would think the port smelled good, I decided to find out more about the origin of this name.

Of course, such a poetic name could be no accident, although its origins remain unclear. The most probable explanation is that Hong Kong was once a center for the production and export of incense, particularly agarwood. As far back as the Ming dynasty, junks would dock at what is now Aberdeen to collect cargoes of incense bound for other Chinese provinces, the rest of Asia, and even Arabia. One of the earliest mentions of the name "Hong Kong" appears on a map in *Yue Daji* ("The Grand Record of Guangdong"), dating from 1595, during the Ming dynasty. It was only with the arrival of the British colonizers in the 1840s that this name stuck and would come to refer to the whole island.

Hong Kong's port was once a center for producing and exporting incense.

Every time I return to Hong Kong, there is one ritual I feel obligated to perform: to cross the harbor on the Star Ferry, one of the city's most iconic forms of transportation. Admittedly, land reclamation has shortened the crossing, making it quicker than before, but I still prefer this route to the tunnels or the MTR.[10] There is something irreplaceable about its slow and steady pace, a rare break in the city's frenetic energy. I always try to take it at sunset, when the skyline is illuminated, and the golden light of the glass towers is reflected on the water. The familiar pitching of the ferry is one of the few things that hasn't changed since my childhood, and that feeling reminds me of where I come from.

It suddenly dawned on me why Hong Kong is known as *fook dei* (福地)—"blessed land"—and why I feel incredibly lucky to have grown up there.

---

10. Mass Transit Railway, Hong Kong's subway system.

# BO LO BAO

## PINEAPPLE BUNS (WITHOUT PINEAPPLE)

**Makes 12 buns**
**Preparation time 1 hour**
**Resting time overnight plus 1 hour 15 minutes**
**Cooking time 16 minutes**

**FOR THE CRUST LAYER:**

1 cup (120 g) unsalted butter
⅔ cup (120 g) sugar
2 cups (240 g) all-purpose (plain) flour
3 tablespoons custard powder
¾ teaspoon baking powder
½ teaspoon baking soda (bicarbonate of soda)
¼ teaspoon salt
1 large (UK medium) egg

**FOR THE ROUX (*TANGZHONG*):**

⅓ cup (60 g) bread (strong) flour

**FOR YEAST ACTIVATION:**

⅓ cup (75 ml) milk
¾ teaspoon sugar
½ small cake (10 g) fresh yeast or 1½ teaspoons active dry (fast-action dried) yeast

**FOR THE BREAD DOUGH:**

3½ cups (480 g) bread (strong) flour
¼ cup (50 g) sugar
¼ teaspoon salt
⅓ cup (75 ml) milk
1 extra-large (UK large) egg
2 tablespoons (30 g) unsalted butter

**FOR GLAZING:**

1 egg yolk

**"There is no pineapple in a pineapple bun." If I were to get a dollar for every time I had to repeat that sentence at my coffee shop while trying to sell one, I would probably be a millionaire by now. The pineapple bun, or *bo lo bao* in Cantonese, owes its name to its texture, which resembles the rough skin of a pineapple. Although it may sound insignificant, it's probably one of the things I miss most about Hong Kong, which is why every bite brings a wave of nostalgia. *(Davina)***

The previous day, prepare the crust layer by mixing the softened butter and sugar thoroughly (using your hands is the quickest way). Mix together the flour, custard powder, baking powder, baking soda, and salt. Add the dry ingredients to the butter-and-sugar mixture and use your hands to combine until the texture resembles that of wet sand. Incorporate the egg. Cover the dough with plastic wrap and refrigerate overnight.

Make the roux: Whisk ⅔ cup (150 ml) water with the flour in a saucepan until smooth. Place the saucepan over medium-high heat and continue to whisk until the mixture thickens to form a smooth paste. Transfer the roux to a bowl, cover with plastic wrap, and let cool for at least 20 minutes.

To activate the yeast, lightly warm the milk, then stir in the sugar and yeast until dissolved. Cover and let rest for 5 minutes. The mixture is ready when it swells and bubbles form.

To make the dough, mix the flour, sugar, and salt. In a separate bowl, whisk together the milk, egg, roux, and activated yeast. Add the mixture to the flour and mix well with a spatula or your hands. The dough will be sticky, but resist the urge to add more flour. Cover with a cloth and let rest for 15 minutes.

After resting, the dough should be less sticky. Fold the dough on itself several times, then gather into a ball. Cut the butter into small pieces and knead into the butter with your hands to incorporate. The dough may become sticky again. Cover with a cloth and let rest for 15 minutes.

After this second rest, fold the dough several more times, gather into a smooth ball, and let rise overnight in the refrigerator.

The next day, divide the dough into 12 equal pieces. If it is still sticky, oil your hands. Shape each dough into a smooth ball.

Arrange the dough balls on a baking sheet lined with parchment (baking) paper, spacing well apart, because they will swell a great deal. Cover and proof for 20 minutes.

Preheat the oven to 325°F (160°C) in fan-assisted (convection) mode or to 350°F (180°C/Gas Mark 4) in static mode.

Take the crust mixture out of the refrigerator 10 minutes before use. Divide into 12 equal pieces and roll each piece into a ball. Place the balls between two sheets of parchment paper and flatten into disks about $\frac{1}{16}$ inch (1 mm) thick. Place one disk on a dough ball. Brush the buns with beaten egg yolk and bake for 16 minutes.

For an authentic feel of Hong Kong, lay a good chunk of butter on each bun before serving.

# 滑蛋菠蘿包



# PINEAPPLE BUN BREAKFAST SANDWICH

**Serves 2**
**Preparation time 10 minutes**
**Cooking time 5 minutes**

2 pineapple buns
½ teaspoon cornstarch (cornflour)
1 tablespoon evaporated milk
4 eggs
1 pinch salt
1 pinch pepper
4 slices cheddar cheese
Vegetable oil

**In recent years, *cha chaan tengs* have come up with the ultimate breakfast: the scrambled egg sandwich made with a pineapple bun. It offers a perfect balance of taste and texture, with the crunchiness of the pineapple bun complementing the softness of the scrambled eggs. *(Davina)***

Halve the buns by cutting them through the center.

Dissolve the cornstarch in the evaporated milk. Add the eggs and 1 teaspoon oil, season with the salt and pepper, and whisk until smooth.

Heat 1 tablespoon oil in a skillet (frying pan) over medium-high heat for 15 to 30 seconds. Quickly whisk the eggs again and add to the skillet. As soon as the edges start to bubble, wait about 5 seconds, then turn off the heat. Using a spatula, gently push the cooked edges toward the center, letting the raw egg cook in turn. Continue until everything is cooked through (the eggs should remain glossy).

Divide the eggs and cover the bottom halves of the buns. Top with 2 cheese slices each. You can add or even substitute the eggs with other ingredients, such as Spam,® ham, or *char siu* (see page 68).

Cover with the tops of the buns and serve immediately.

# GAI MEI BAO

## COCKTAIL BUNS

**Makes 10 buns**
**Preparation time 30 minutes**
**Resting time 2 hours 45 minutes**
**Cooking time 20 minutes**

**FOR THE ROUX (*TANGZHONG*):**

25 g bread (strong) flour

**FOR THE DOUGH:**

2½ cups (350 g) bread (strong) flour
¼ cup (50 g) sugar
⅙ small cake (3.5 g) fresh yeast or ¾ teaspoon active dry (fast-action dried) yeast
½ egg
3 tablespoons (40 g) unsalted butter

**FOR THE FILLING:**

3½ tablespoons (50 g) unsalted butter
1 egg
3½ tablespoons (40 g) sugar
1½ tablespoons (25 g) custard powder
½ cup plus 1 tablespoon (40 g) instant dry (powdered) milk
1¼ cups (100 g) shredded coconut
½ teaspoon vegetable oil

**FOR THE TOPPING:**

1¾ tablespoons (25 g) unsalted butter, softened
3¾ teaspoons (15 g) sugar
2 tablespoons (15 g) cake (Italian '00') flour

**FOR GLAZING:**

1 egg
White sesame seeds
Simple syrup

**There's something almost magical about these sweet buns—an alchemy that transforms coconut, sugar, and butter into a delicacy that far exceeds the sum of its ingredients. As it cooks, the coconut softens and blends with the other ingredients, creating a rich, slightly sweet, and incredibly creamy filling. *(Davina)***

To make the roux, whisk ⅓ cup plus 1½ tablespoons (100 ml) water with the flour in a saucepan until smooth. Put over medium heat and stir the mixture continuously until thick and smooth. Let cool.

To make the dough, mix together the flour, sugar, roux, and yeast. Add the half egg and mix until incorporated. Gradually stir in ⅓ cup plus 1½ tablespoons (100 ml) water until smooth. Add the butter and knead until completely incorporated.

Transfer the dough to a lightly floured surface and knead until soft and elastic. To test if the dough has been kneaded enough, take a small piece and stretch it: it should become thin and translucent without tearing. Place the dough in an oiled bowl, cover, and let rise in a warm place for 1 hour 30 minutes to 2 hours.

To make the filling, melt the butter. Beat the egg until smooth. Add the sugar and melted butter, then gradually incorporate the custard powder and instant milk. Add the shredded coconut and oil, then mix to combine.

To make the topping, cream the butter with the sugar until smooth, then incorporate the flour. Transfer the mixture to a pastry (piping) bag (or use a freezer bag and cut a small opening in a corner).

Once the dough has risen, knead on a floured surface for 5 minutes to remove any air bubbles. Divide the dough into 10 equal pieces. Flatten each piece into an oval measuring about 4¾ by 3¼ inches (12 × 8 cm) and ¼ inch (5 mm) thick. Place a heaping tablespoon of filling in the center. Roll up the dough into a tube around the filling, tucking in the ends to completely encase.

Place the buns on a baking sheet lined with parchment (baking) paper. Cover with a damp cloth and proof for 30 to 45 minutes.

Preheat the oven to 350°F (175°C/Gas Mark 4).

Brush the buns with a thin coating of beaten egg. Using the pastry bag, pipe 2 lines of topping on each bun. Sprinkle all over with sesame seeds.

Bake for 17 to 20 minutes, until the buns turn golden brown. As soon as they come out of the oven, brush with syrup for a glossy effect.

# 奶醬多
# CONDENSED MILK AND PEANUT BUTTER TOAST

**Serves 2**
**Preparation time 5 minutes**

2 slices sandwich bread
1 tablespoon (15 g) butter
4 tablespoons peanut butter
2 tablespoons condensed milk

Toast the bread. Spread the toast with butter, then with peanut butter. Drizzle over the condensed milk and serve immediately.

# PENG CHAU
## *ADA*

I discovered this small island across from Lantau by chance on a particularly sunny day.

Taking advantage of the 40-minute ferry ride from Pier No. 6 at Central to do a little research, I found that it covered an area of about ¼ acre (1 $km^2$) and had around 6,000 inhabitants. As soon as I disembarked, it became obvious it was a refuge, a haven of calm, a village outside of the big city.

For a start, there are no cars on Peng Chau; everyone travels by foot or bicycle. There are bikes chained to every tree, every post, and every wooden bench, some with a basket on the handlebars, and some with a child's seat. There are no 50-story towers lining the waterfront; just small, colorful buildings and a single supermarket. It's quiet, and the people there are relaxed. You might think you were in a Dutch village, or somewhere in Italy, or in a Miyazaki movie—maybe a little of all three.

Then I passed a few small eateries (the specialty here is pineapple bun with ice cream), a bakery, a store selling fabric, and another selling toys and stationery. Behind the counter of a stall selling rubber key rings and pencils was an old man watching television, his feet propped up on a chair. There were no signs of souvenir shops selling "Peng Chau" magnets or stickers, an indication that tourists were few and far between. On the left, my attention was drawn to what seemed to be a dark alleyway with a large sign graffitied on a wall that read "Leather Factory."

I stepped inside and noticed that there were circles of cardboard cups hanging from the ceiling. It was an art piece. As I emerged from the alley, I discovered an almost indescribable place: an eclectic mix of old recycled objects decorated what had obviously once been a small leather factory, with workshops now been turned into a shop selling old pottery or a tiny café. Its walls were covered with blue, red, and yellow graffiti; and an assortment of old objects adorned trees and poles.

You might think you were in a Dutch village, or somewhere in Italy, or in a Miyazaki movie.

More than a tourist attraction and exhibition space, the Leather Factory is a vestige of a bygone era, of the 1970s when the island of Peng Chau was still home to industry. The following decades saw the economy shift to the services sector, leading to the closure of most island industries and the people of Peng Chau finding work on Hong Kong Island. The only remaining businesses were those supplying the local population of the island: food, restaurants, some furniture, supplies, and stationery. Although the owners of these businesses would mostly be counting on their children to take over, they, in turn, preferred to live in the city, where there are greater opportunities and prosperity. These aging shopkeepers have continued to keep the local economy going—sometimes to earn a living, and sometimes to keep up social ties—but never at the risk of their personal well-being. As a result, it isn't unusual when walking along the two shopping streets to see a few shuttered storefronts with a sign written in Chinese characters saying "closed for a few days." The islanders' relationship with time, work, and health is different: shopkeepers won't think twice about closing if they feel too tired, if it's too hot, or if they have an appointment. The priority here, unlike in the rest of Hong Kong, is not to earn as much money as possible but to enjoy life, the island, and the bonds formed with other inhabitants of the island. Even newcomers will usually acclimatize to this more fluid way of living and working.

TTS
HK
24 x 400 ML
COCONUT MILK

# SAI DOR SI

## HONG KONG-STYLE FRENCH TOAST

**Serves 4**
**Preparation time 5 minutes**
**Cooking time 5 minutes per sandwich**

1 loaf sandwich bread, unsliced
4 tablespoons peanut butter
3 eggs
1¼ cups (300 ml) vegetable oil
4 tablespoons (60 g) butter
¼ cup (60 ml) condensed milk

**French toast, which has nothing in common with the version that is made in France, is to Hong Kong what pancakes are to New York.**

Cut 8 thick slices from the loaf of bread.

Spread 4 slices with 2 heaping tablespoons peanut butter. Cover with the remaining 4 slices to make sandwiches. Cut off the crusts.

Beat the eggs in a bowl and lightly soak the sandwiches in the beaten eggs. Don't soak the sandwiches for too long or they will be difficult to handle.

Heat the oil in a large skillet (frying pan) and fry the sandwiches first on their edges (about 30 seconds on each side), then on their flat surfaces (1 minute 30 seconds on each side). Drain on paper towels (kitchen paper).

Serve warm, topped with a pat (knob) of butter and drizzled with 1 tablespoon of condensed milk.

# LAI CHA / YUENYEUNG

## MILK TEA / COFFEE MILK TEA

**Serves 3 to 4**
**Preparation time 5 minutes**
**Cooking time 5 minutes**
**Steeping time 10 minutes**

⅓ cup (30 g) Ceylon tea
¼ cup (20 g) orange pekoe tea
2 cups (500 ml) evaporated milk
1¼ cups (300 ml) black coffee
Sugar

**Being a former British colony, it should not be a surprise that milk tea has become an essential part of Hong Kong's food culture. However, like many local dishes, it has evolved over time as a result of limited access to ingredients—fresh milk often being replaced by evaporated milk—and local tastes, allowing it to take on an identity of its own. Hong Kong-style milk tea is also known as *see mut lai cha*, which translates as "silk stocking milk tea." The name refers to the sock- or stockinglike filter bag used to strain the tea, but it also alludes to the smooth and velvety texture resulting from this way of making it. Although there's generous consensus on how Hong Kong milk tea should taste, every *cha chaan teng* or *dai pai dong* has its own recipe, often handed down from generation to generation. The different flavors of the milk tea served come from the blend of teas used, which is why, unsurprisingly, those serving the tea keep their particular combination a closely guarded secret. Nevertheless, most have Ceylon tea as the basic component, with variations incorporating other varieties, such as pu'erh or Earl Grey, depending on the recipe. Having lived away from home for a long time, I experimented with several blends and was finally able to replicate one of my favorite Hong Kong milk teas, which balances floral and earthy tones with the creamy sweetness of milk. Feel free to experiment with different proportions and tea varieties. You can also give this drink a new dimension by transforming it into *yuenyeung*, which combines Hong Kong-style milk tea with coffee. The Cantonese name *yuenyeung* actually refers to mandarin ducks, which are reputed to mate for life and are seen as the symbol for union in Chinese culture. In this case, it is a poetic way of highlighting the balance of two distinct flavors: the sweet richness of milk tea and the bold intensity of coffee.**

Put the loose tea leaves into a milk tea filter bag or tea infuser and place inside a saucepan. Add 4¼ cups (1 liter) water and bring to a boil over medium heat. Turn off the heat and let steep (infuse) for 10 minutes.

Drain the filter or infuser and place it in a second saucepan. Carefully transfer the brewed tea from the first saucepan into the second one. Repeat this process 2 or 3 times to oxygenate the tea, releasing its aroma and enhancing its flavor.

Reheat the tea and bring to a boil one last time. Your tea base is ready.

To make Hong Kong-style milk tea, fill a cup three-quarters full with evaporated milk, then top off with the tea base. Mix well and sweeten as desired. This drink can be enjoyed hot or iced.

To make *yuenyeung*, brew black coffee (fairly strong) by your preferred method. Fill a cup three-quarters full with milk tea, then top off with the coffee. This drink can also be enjoyed hot or iced.

# SHEUNG WAN AND DRIED SEAFOOD

## *DAVINA*

Whenever I go back to Hong Kong, I ask my friends if there is anything they would like me to bring back for them. The reply is typically a polite "no thanks," but requests come every so often for dried seafood. It's only recently that I have discovered just how expensive these products can be. When I was little, I would grimace as I passed those stores, attempting to avoid the strong sea smell that lingered in the air. I had no idea at the time that they were among the city's most prized culinary treasures.

Of course, not all dried seafood costs a fortune. Dried shrimp and scallops are a staple of Cantonese cuisine and add a touch of umami and the characteristic fragrance of the ocean to everyday dishes. There are also the luxury products, including abalone, sea cucumber, and swim bladder. These are the Hong Kong equivalents of caviar and foie gras. Their price can reach thousands of dollars per kilogram, depending on their size and origin.

Such is the importance of dried seafood to Hong Kong's culinary identity that an entire street in the Sheung Wan district is dedicated to it. Dried Seafood Street stretches from Des Voeux Road West to Wing Lok Street and Bonham Strand West. In store after store, each with its own know-how and specialties, vendors offer different types of dried seafood.

As well as dried seafood, these stores sell a host of other dried ingredients, such as mushrooms and different meats, as well as medicinal products, such as ginkgo seeds and yellow mushrooms, which are often used in soups and desserts. One ingredient that always made me laugh as a child was *fat choy*, which literally means "hair vegetable." As its name suggests, it looks like a tuft of tangled black hair. *Fat choy* is often a feature of the menu at Chinese New Year, because its name is homophonous with the Cantonese expression *fat choy* (發財), meaning "to grow rich" and symbolizing prosperity. However, despite its cultural significance, I couldn't help laughing when my mother suggested I eat hair.

As you leave Dried Seafood Street, you soon realize that Sheung Wan is a neighborhood with a little of everything. A few blocks away is Man Mo Temple, worthy of a visit, which is located just above Upper Lascar Row, also known as Antique Street. Here, stalls overflow with treasures from another time—china, vintage alarm clocks, and retro posters, to name a few. It makes a fascinating contrast to the neighborhood's other facet comprising gourmet restaurants, specialty cafés, and contemporary art galleries.

Sheung Wan is a neighborhood where history and modernity are in constant dialogue. A unique energy can be felt here, a blend of old and new that will captivate you on your first visit. It's one of those places that you can never tire of, no matter how many times you return.

In store after store, each with its own know-how and specialties, vendors offer different types of dried seafood.

200

# 沙嗲牛肉麵

# SATAY BEEF NOODLES

**Serves 2**
**Preparation time 30 minutes**
**Marinating time 1 hour**
**Cooking time 20 minutes**

7 ounces (200 g) flap (flank) steak
2 tablespoons vegetable oil
2 cloves garlic
1 shallot
1 teaspoon curry powder
2 packages instant noodles
Scallions (spring onions)

**FOR THE MARINADE:**
1 teaspoon light soy sauce
½ teaspoon dark soy sauce
1 tablespoon oyster sauce
½ teaspoon sugar
2 teaspoons cornstarch (cornflour)
1 teaspoon white pepper
1 medium (UK large) egg
2 teaspoons sesame oil

**FOR THE SATAY SAUCE:**
3 tablespoons sha cha sauce
2 tablespoons peanut butter
1 tablespoon oyster sauce
1 teaspoon light soy sauce
1 teaspoon dark soy sauce
1 teaspoon shrimp paste

**In Hong Kong, satay beef noodles are eaten for breakfast. For us, there's nothing more satisfying than a bowl of piping hot instant noodles served with a ladle of thick satay sauce just spicy enough to wake us up and get us ready for the day. *(Davina)***

Thinly slice the beef against the grain and put it into a large bowl. Add the marinade ingredients with 2 tablespoons of water and mix well. Cover and marinate for 1 hour.

Mix all the satay sauce ingredients in a bowl with ½ cup (120 ml) water.

Heat the oil in a large skillet (frying pan) over medium-high heat, then cook the marinated beef for 5 minutes and set aside.

In the same skillet, sauté the finely chopped garlic and shallot over medium heat. Add 1 tablespoon oil, if necessary. Stir in the curry powder and cook for another 2 minutes.

Add the sauce and mix well. Reduce the heat to low and let simmer for 10 minutes. Return the meat to the skillet and cook for another 5 minutes over low heat.

Cook the instant noodles according to the package directions. Transfer to a bowl, cover with a ladle of satay beef, and top with scallions.

# 蛋牛治
# CORNED BEEF EGG SANDWICH

**Serves 2**
**Preparation time 5 minutes**
**Cooking time 5 minutes**

4 slices sandwich bread
4 slices corned beef
3½ tablespoons (50 ml) vegetable oil
6 eggs
1 tablespoon light soy sauce
Salt and pepper

**The scrambled egg and corned beef sandwich is traditional Hong Kong breakfast fare. It's probably the easiest thing to make whenever I miss Hong Kong and crave a flavor that will remind me of gulping down my breakfast while sitting on a plastic chair somewhere in Sheung Wan. *(Ada)***

Cut the crusts off the bread. Cut the corned beef into strips.

Heat 1 tablespoon oil in a skillet (frying pan) over medium heat and brown the corned beef for a few minutes.

In the meantime, briskly beat the eggs with the soy sauce. Add the corned beef.

Add the remaining oil to the skillet and heat through, watching carefully. As soon as the oil begins to smoke, immediately turn off the heat and add the eggs to the pan. Using a silicone spatula, quickly push the edges of the eggs in toward the center. Repeat until cooked (but not overcooked).

Spread the eggs over 2 slices of bread, close the sandwiches, season with salt and pepper, and serve immediately.

# CONGEE

## RICE PORRIDGE

**Serves 4**
**Preparation time 15 minutes**
**Soaking time overnight**
**Cooking time 1 hour 30 minutes**

- 1 cup (185 g) white rice
- 1 chicken bouillon (stock) cube
- 2 scallions (spring onions)
- 1¼-inch (3-cm) length fresh ginger
- 3½ ounces (100 g) ground (minced) pork
- ¼ cup (60 ml) light soy sauce
- ¼ cup (60 ml) sesame oil

**A rice porridge used in traditional Chinese medicine for its digestive benefits, largely because of the starch in the rice, congee is most often enjoyed at breakfast, but can also be eaten when you feel unwell—or hungover. *(Ada)***

The previous day, soak the rice in a bowl of water.

On the actual day, rinse the rice until the water runs clear. Put the rice into a pot with the bouillon cube and 10 times its volume in water (1 part rice to 10 parts water), then bring to a boil. Stir well. Cover the pot halfway with the lid, and let cook for 1 hour to 1 hour 30 minutes. Stir regularly to keep the rice from sticking to the bottom of the pot.

In the meantime, chop the scallions. Peel and slice the ginger into thin strips.

About 20 minutes before the end of the cooking time, break up the ground pork and add to the rice. The congee is ready when the rice becomes thick, creamy, and glossy.

Divide the congee into 4 large bowls, garnish with ginger and scallions, and add 1 tablespoon soy sauce and 1 tablespoon sesame oil to each bowl. Serve hot.

### VARIATIONS

Feel free to vary this dish by adding seasonal vegetables of your choice. I love to add corn for the comforting sweetness and crunchy texture that contrasts with the creaminess of the congee.

# SAVORY SOY MILK

7 A.M. / 9 A.M.

**Serves 4**
**Preparation time 10 minutes**
**Resting time overnight**
**Cooking time 1 hour**

1⅓ cups (250 g) dried soybeans
1 teaspoon fine salt

**Naturally, you can buy soy milk at the supermarket, add a little salt, and heat it up for breakfast. But it won't taste the same; nor will it give you the tremendous satisfaction of having created something from start to finish.** ***(Ada)***

The previous day, rinse the soybeans two times. Put them into a large bowl, cover with plenty of water, and soak overnight.

On the actual day, rinse the swollen soybeans again. Add to a saucepan with 12¾ cups (3 liters) of water and bring to a boil. Reduce the heat and cook for 10 to 15 minutes.

Transfer the water and soybeans to a blender (do this in 2 batches, if necessary) and blend well until milky.

Return the soy milk to the pan and simmer for 30 minutes, stirring continuously and keep an eye on it—like cow milk, soy milk has a tendency to boil over with little warning.

Add the salt and simmer for another 10 minutes.

Strain the soy milk through cheesecloth (muslin) before serving.

## VARIATIONS

If you prefer a sweet version, substitute the salt with 2 tablespoons of sugar and 1 pinch of salt.

# YAU CHAR KWAI

## DOUGHNUT STICKS

**Makes 5**
**Preparation time 30 minutes**
**Resting time 30 minutes plus overnight**
**Cooking time 15 minutes**

- 1⅔ cups 200 g all-purpose (plain) flour
- ⅓ teaspoon (2 g) salt
- ½ teaspoon (2 g) baking soda (bicarbonate of soda)
- 1½ teaspoons (6 g) baking powder
- 1 tablespoon vegetable oil
- 1 teaspoon white vinegar
- Oil for deep-frying

**If you were to ask me what I would consider a typical Hong Kong breakfast, I would have to include *yau char kwai*. These crisp, airy, and slightly alkaline-tasting, deep-fried doughnut sticks are often dipped in a bowl of steaming congee or savory soy milk. *(Davina)***

The previous day, mix the flour with the salt, baking soda, baking powder, oil, and vinegar in a bowl. Gradually add ½ cup (115 ml) of water while stirring continuously.

Transfer the dough to a stand mixer and knead for 15 minutes. Cover and let rest for 30 minutes.

On a lightly floured work surface, roll out the dough into a long rectangle measuring about 1 by 4 inches (2.5 × 10 cm). Brush with oil and cover in plastic wrap (clingfilm). Refrigerate overnight.

In the morning, take the dough out of the refrigerator and let rest at room temperature until it is completely relaxed and soft to the touch.

Heat frying oil in a pot to 325°F (160°C). If you don't have a thermometer, dip a chopstick into the oil. It is hot enough when bubbles start to form around it.

Unwrap the dough and cut into 10 equal strips.

Lay one dough strip on top of another and press lengthwise with a chopstick so the two stick together. Repeat the operation with the remaining strips, dusting with flour, if necessary.

Carefully stretch each piece of dough and place in the hot oil. Fry the sticks one at a time to keep them from burning. Use chopsticks to turn the sticks gently until completely puffed and golden brown, then drain the excess oil on paper towels (kitchen paper).

*Yau char kwai* are best eaten warm, but they can be kept in the refrigerator for up to 3 days. Reheat in a skillet (frying pan) over low heat, turning them several times.

# CHOW MEIN

## FRIED NOODLES

**Serves 4**
**Preparation time 15 minutes**
**Cooking time 10 minutes**

1 clove garlic
2 scallions (spring onions)
100 g bean sprouts
400 g chow mein noodles
Vegetable oil

**FOR THE SAUCE:**
1 teaspoon cornstarch (cornflour)
2 tablespoons light soy sauce
1 tablespoon mirin
2 tablespoons oyster sauce
1 teaspoon sugar
1 teaspoon sesame oil

To make the sauce, mix the cornstarch with the soy sauce and mirin. Add the remaining sauce ingredients and mix until combined.

Peel and mince (very finely chop) the garlic. Wash the scallions, separate the white bulbs from the green leaves, and chop both. Wash the bean sprouts.

Cook the noodles according to the package directions.

Sauté the garlic and white part of the scallions in a wok. Add the noodles, followed by the sauce, and stir-fry briskly over high heat for a few minutes. Add the bean sprouts, stir-fry for another 2 minutes, then serve hot, sprinkled with the chopped scallion leaves.

# THE FOREIGN, PARTICULARLY BRITISH, INFLUENCES ON HONG KONG CUISINE

## *ADA*

Is this more obvious in Hong Kong than elsewhere, or have I simply become more interested in the food culture of this city than that of any other? Everyday food in Hong Kong is a veritable manifestation of the migrations that form a part of its history.

Hong Kong was originally a fishing village. It is now a strategic port for ships plying the route between Europe and Asia. Here, they take on supplies and rest their crews as a halfway point on long ocean voyages.

Following the Cultural Revolution in the People's Republic of China, Hong Kong's population exploded in the 1950s and 1960s. It was also a period of industrialization and the rise of manufacturing. To meet the need for quick meals during the long working days and inflation-squeezed household budgets, there was an explosion of *cha chaan tengs*—Hong Kong's version of diners or cafés—which offered low-price products imported directly from Europe, thanks to the British presence.

Hong Kong was originally a fishing village. It is now a strategic port for ships plying the route between Europe and Asia.

The British also imported spices from their other colonies through the Indian, Bangladeshi, and Pakistani workers who went to Hong Kong to provide manual labor (for example, in construction). This is evident in the curry dishes that would develop in Hong Kong, including curry fish balls and beef brisket curry.

The 1960s also saw the advent of soy sauce Western restaurants. Founded by a generation of chefs who had traveled to the West to study the art of Western-style cooking, these establishments follow the codes of traditional European restaurants, with their waiters in black and white uniforms, tablecloths, tray service, and—most important—menus featuring the essentials of Western cuisine. Although the popularity of steak with pepper sauce, Cobb salad, and soufflés may be declining these days, they are still emblematic of this cuisine.

The contemporary food scene in Hong Kong is highly globalized. There are Italian, Indian, French, Vietnamese, and Thai restaurants everywhere. In addition, as wages soared, the number of *cha chaan tengs* in the city also declined. The new generations prefer to work in the service sector to earn a better living, and both *cha chaan tengs* and *dai pa dongs*, which cater more to the working classes, are closing down one at a time.

的士上落客除外

# 火腿通粉
# MACARONI AND HAM SOUP

**Serves 2**
**Preparation time 10 minutes**
**Cooking time 15 minutes**

5 ounces (140 g) elbow macaroni
1¼ cups (300 ml) chicken broth (stock)
4 slices Spam®
2 pinches white pepper

**The best place to try this dish is the Australia Dairy Company, a Kowloon institution. Opened in 1970, this eatery owes its name to the fact that its founder worked on a farm in Australia in the 1940s. It is one of the most iconic *cha chaan tengs* in Hong Kong, a place people line up to enjoy the city's most famous breakfasts. It is particularly renowned for its creamy and delicious eggs. Similar to all *cha chaan tengs*, you sit down quickly, eat quickly, and leave quickly so that your table can be taken by the next hungry customers in the long line. *(Ada)***

Cook the macaroni according to the package directions and drain.

In a pot, dilute the stock with scant 1 cup (200 ml) water and put over medium heat.

Slice the Spam®.

Divide the macaroni and hot broth between 2 bowls, then add the Spam® and season each soup with a pinch of white pepper.

VARIATIONS

You can replace the Spam® with cooked ham.

11 AM / 2 PM

# 午餐

# BING SUTTS, CHA CHAAN TENGS, AND DAI PAI DONGS

## *DAVINA*

Don't worry too much about any confusion you might have; it also took me a while to understand the difference between a *bing sutt*, a *cha chaan teng*, and a *dai pai dong*, even as a local. Today, their offerings tend to overlap, blurring the distinction even further. It wasn't until I was looking for a name for my café in Paris that I actually looked into the definition of these establishments, which is how I came up with Bing Sutt.

One of the questions people ask me most often at my café is "What does Bing Sutt mean?" The literal translation of the term is "ice room." Taken out of context, this may seem to be strange, but the origin of *bing sutts* offers a perfect explanation.

*Bing sutts* first appeared in the 1880s as establishments for the wealthy who could afford the luxury of iced drinks—a veritable relief during Hong Kong's sweltering summers. In those days, blocks of ice were imported from Europe, which made them extremely valuable. However, as local ice cream factories were set up in the mid-twentieth century, at a time when few households owned a refrigerator, *bing sutts* became popular places for cooling refreshments.

I've enjoyed some of my best meals at these street stalls.

At the time, local regulations required *bing sutts* to serve only drinks, sandwiches, and snacks that did not require baking or frying. This restriction, coupled with consumers' growing purchasing power in the 1950s, gave rise to *cha chaan tengs*, diner-style establishments serving a fusion of Chinese and Western food. They are home to some of Hong Kong's iconic dishes, such as milk tea, egg tarts, Hong Kong-style spaghetti Bolognese, and even our own version of borsch (I always find it funny to see people's reactions of disbelief when I tell them we also make borsch in Hong Kong).

This culinary mosaic also includes *dai pai dongs*, which gained in popularity after World War II. *Dai pai dong* is an expression that means "big license stall," in reference to the special permits that were granted to the families of civil servants who were wounded or killed during the war. The aim of this initiative was to enable them to legalize their food vending businesses.

I've enjoyed some of my best meals at these street stalls, which can typically be described as a few folding tables, plastic stools, and a small kitchen set up in the open air. Unfortunately, such experiences are becoming increasingly rare, because there are fewer than 30 *dai pai dongs* left in Hong Kong today. Since the 1970s, complaints about smoke, noise, and traffic jams have led the government to no longer issue new licenses. Today, existing licenses can be passed on to only a spouse or the next generation.

6B
6A

# CHOW FAN

## FRIED RICE

**Serves 4**
**Preparation time 15 minutes**
**Cooking time 10 minutes**

4 scallions (spring onions)
2 cloves garlic
1 carrot
1 small can corn kernels
¼ cup (60 ml) vegetable oil
⅔ cup (100 g) peas
1⅓ cups (200 g) cold cooked rice

**FOR THE SAUCE:**
1 tablespoon light soy sauce
1 tablespoon cooking sake
1 tablespoon oyster sauce
1 teaspoon white pepper

Chop the scallions and garlic. Peel and dice the carrot. Drain the corn.

Heat the oil in a wok. Remove the wok from the heat, add the scallions (to keep them from burning), and stir for 2 minutes. Remove the scallions and some of the oil, then add the garlic and vegetables and return the wok to the heat. Sauté for 5 minutes over medium heat. Increase the heat, add 1 tablespoon of the scallion-flavored cooking oil, and stir in the rice. Sauté for another 3 to 4 minutes, stirring continuously to keep the contents of the wok from burning.

Combine the sauce ingredients and add to the rice, stirring for a few more minutes.

Finally, add the scallions, cook for another 2 minutes, and serve hot.

### NOTE

The wok must be hot when you add the rice, because if the temperature is too cool, it will release starch and turn mushy.

# THE FIRE DRAGON OF TAI HANG
## *DAVINA*

Having been raised in Hong Kong, I'm a city girl at heart. I grew up with the energy and fast pace of urban life, with the constant sense that there was something new to discover around every corner. But age has taught me to appreciate peace and quiet, which may be why Tai Hang has become one of my favorite neighborhoods.

Set back a few streets away from the buzz of Causeway Bay, Tai Hang offers a moment of tranquility in the heart of Hong Kong. This charming district combines independent cafés, small local restaurants, and historic sites, which draw a constant stream of visitors and regulars. As you stroll along its quiet, narrow streets, you should come across traditional open-air food stalls, such as Bing Kee, famous for its crispy pork noodles. However, if you continue to walk a short distance, you're sure to find a trendy place serving specialty coffees and the latest fads in pastries.

Once a year, during the Mid-Autumn Festival, this usually peaceful neighborhood comes alive with a totally distinct energy. Thousands of visitors flock to see the Fire Dragon Dance, now listed as a National Intangible Cultural Heritage. I have had the opportunity to experience this fascinating spectacle only once, as a child perched on my mother's shoulders and trying to see over the crowd, but the memory is forever engraved on my mind.

The dragon's eyes are painted in, a ritual that symbolizes their opening and breathing life into the dragon.

The parade starts at a temple known as Lin Fa Kung, which means "Lotus Flower Palace." There, the dragon's eyes are painted in, a ritual that symbolizes their opening and breathing life into the dragon. The 200-foot (67-m)-long creature makes its way through the narrow streets of Tai Hang, illuminated by about 12,000 burning incense sticks, which are then distributed to the crowd as a blessing and good-luck charm.

This exhilarating celebration perfectly embodies the community spirit that makes Tai Hang so unique. This neighborhood is undeniably a microcosm of Hong Kong, a perfect example of how cultural heritage and contemporary influences can coexist to form a unique identity.

本苑不設
訪客車位
SX
5469

京街12號
No.12 King Street
的士 TAXI
的士

NO.4 KING STREET

11 A.M. / 2 P.M.

# CANTONESE POACHED CHICKEN

**Serves 4 to 6**
**Preparation time 15 minutes**
**Cooking time 50 minutes**

2 tablespoons kosher (coarse) salt

1 whole pasture-raised (free-range) chicken* (about 5½ pounds/2.5 kg)

**FOR THE SAUCE:**

2-inch (5-cm) length fresh ginger

½ bunch scallions (spring onions)

⅓ cup plus 1½ tablespoons (100 ml) vegetable oil

1 teaspoon salt

2 tablespoons sesame oil

* The chicken should be as fresh as possible. Traditionally, the chicken is served with its head and legs, a guarantee of good luck for the entire year ahead, from beginning (head) to end (legs).

Bring a large pot of water to a boil with the kosher salt.

To prepare the chicken, stretch and pull the legs away from the body (without separating—the aim is to create a cavity). Pierce a hole through the skin at the nape of the neck. Plunge the chicken 3 times into the boiling water. This will help to distribute the heat evenly. Next, submerge the chicken completely into the water (nothing should stick out). Cover the pot. Boil for 5 minutes, then reduce the heat and let simmer for about 45 minutes.

In the meantime, make the sauce. Peel and mince (very finely chop) the ginger. Mince the white scallion bulbs.

In a small saucepan, heat the vegetable oil to a simmer and add the ginger. Cook for just under 1 minute, then add the scallion bulbs. Cook the ginger and scallions for about 15 seconds, transfer to a bowl, and set aside. The purpose of this step is to release their aromas. Add the salt and sesame oil, mix well, then taste and adjust the seasoning as needed. You can also vary the amount of scallion and ginger according to your preference.

Once the chicken is cooked, drain and immediately plunge it into a bowl of ice water to stop the cooking process. This is an important step, because it keeps the chicken from drying out: it traps the cooking juices in the meat, making it more tender.

# WONTON MEIN

## WONTON NOODLE SOUP

**Serves 4**
**Preparation time 15 minutes**
**Cooking time 1 hour 30 minutes for the broth plus 2 minutes**
**Resting time 30 minutes**

1 package wonton (thin egg) noodles
½ bunch fresh cilantro (coriander)

**FOR THE BROTH:**

14 ounces (400 g) pork Boston butt (collar or neck)
10½ ounces (300 g) pork chops
2-inch (5-cm) length fresh ginger
1 bunch scallions (spring onion)
1 tablespoon salt
1 tablespoon dried fish roe*
1 tablespoon mirin
1 tablespoon light soy sauce

* This ingredient may be hard to find outside Hong Kong. If you are unable find it at an Asian grocery store, omit the ingredient.

**FOR THE WONTONS:**

16 large raw shrimp (prawns), peeled
½ egg
1 tablespoon sesame oil
1 pinch salt
1 pinch white pepper
16 wonton wrappers

**In the 1920s, Mak Woon-Chi was renowned throughout his hometown of Guangzhou as the "King of Wonton Noodle." In the 1940s, he passed on his knowledge to his son, Mak King-Hun, who then moved to Hong Kong. In 1968, Mak King-Hun opened his first *dai pa dong* in Central, called Mak Un-Kee ("Skinny Mak," which was his nickname). Today, Mak's Noodle is a Michelin-star chain of more than a dozen restaurants that are beloved by Hong Kongers everywhere. *(Ada)***

To make the broth, put the pork, ginger, white scallion bulbs, salt, and fish roe into a pot and cover with 8½ cups (2 liters) water. Bring to a boil and skim off the scum, then cover the pot halfway with the lid and let simmer for 1 hour 30 minutes. Strain, then add the mirin and soy sauce.

To make the wontons, cut a slit along the backs of the shrimp and remove the black vein. Rinse the shrimp in ice-cold water for several minutes, then drain and wipe dry.

Blend the shrimp with the beaten egg, sesame oil, salt, and pepper to a smooth paste. Refrigerate for 30 minutes.

Add 1 tablespoon of filling to each wonton wrapper, fold the wrapper over the filling, and press to seal. Cook the wontons in boiling water for 1 to 2 minutes, until they float to the surface.

Cook the noodles according to the package directions.

Chop the scallion leaves.

Divide the noodles into 4 bowls, then add 4 wontons and 1 ladle of hot broth to each bowl. Garnish with scallion and cilantro sprigs.

11 A.M. / 2 P.M.

# TOMATO NOODLE SOUP

**Serves 2**
**Preparation time 10 minutes**
**Cooking time 40 minutes**

2 large, ripe tomatoes
1 onion
1 tablespoon vegetable oil
2 tablespoons tomato paste (puree)
4¼ cups (1 liter) chicken broth (stock; or water)
1 tablespoon ketchup
3½ ounces (100 g) instant noodles
Salt and pepper

**The first time I tried tomato noodle soup was something of a challenge for me. On the day in question, I had no desire whatsoever to eat instant noodles for breakfast. However, when that steaming bowl of noodles in their thick and slightly sweet tomato soup was set down in front of me, I wanted to devour the whole thing immediately—and I did.** ***(Ada)***

Wash and dice the tomatoes. Peel and dice the onion.

Sauté the onion in the oil over medium heat for 5 minutes. Add the tomato paste, broth, and tomatoes. Season with salt and pepper and bring to a boil, then reduce the heat and let simmer for 30 to 40 minutes, uncovered to let the water evaporate and the stock thicken.

Add the ketchup and mix to combine. Adjust the seasoning, if necessary—the soup should be slightly sweet and tangy.

Cook the noodles according to the package directions, then serve with the hot soup.

## VARIATIONS

For a more complete breakfast, you can beat 2 eggs, scramble them for 3 minutes in a hot skillet (frying pan), and place on top of the soup.

# *SIU MEI* CANTONESE BARBECUE
## *DAVINA*

If there's one thing I really miss when I'm away from Hong Kong, it's *char siu* (BBQ pork). Tender pieces of Boston butt pork (collar or neck) are marinated in a rich and fragrant sauce and then roasted to perfection. Whether served on its own or in a bowl with steamed jasmine (Thai fragrant) rice, this is my definition of comfort food.

*Siu mei* (燒味), an umbrella term for Cantonese-style barbecued and roasted meat, has become a symbol of Cantonese cuisine around the world. In Hong Kong, it's common to see roasted ducks and crispy pork bellies hanging in restaurant windows, and their fragrance fills the streets. Whether roast goose, *char siu*, or soy sauce chicken, there is nothing simple about *siu mei*. It illustrates all the skill, experience, and knowledge that define Cantonese cuisine.

Cantonese barbecue dates back to the Tang and Song dynasties, a time when trade with China along the Silk Road led to an exchange of ingredients and culinary techniques. The Cantonese quickly adopted and perfected these methods, developing the flavors that would lay the foundations of *siu mei*. One of the key innovations is the rotisserie oven used today to prepare *char siu*, called a *tai hong lo* or "space oven." The marinated *char siu* is first roasted and then glazed, before being put back in the oven for another roasting, which gives it that iconic crispy, caramelized finish.

Over time, chefs have perfected the balance of flavors of Cantonese barbecued meats by combining soy sauce and Chinese five-spice powder to create the rich umami flavor in the meat. What really sets *siu mei* apart from the roasted and barbecued meat of other Chinese regions, however, is their unique sweetness, which is achieved by adding maltose to the glaze. This harmonious blend of sweet, salty, and umami gives Cantonese barbecued meat an irresistible taste.

Today, *siu mei* is so deeply rooted in Hong Kong culture that it has raised the city's profile on the international food scene, highlighted by the recognition given to this culinary tradition by the Michelin Guide. Whenever someone asks me what they must try in Hong Kong, I give them my list of restaurants specializing in *siu sei*. More than just a meal, *siu mei* is a part of my heritage and a source of pride for me. Whenever I make a journey back to Hong Kong, I know that as soon as I arrive, my mother will be waiting for me at home with a plate of *char siu* on the table for lunch.

There is nothing simple about *siu mei*. It illustrates all the skill, experience, and knowledge that define Cantonese cuisine.

生意興隆
燒鴨
半隻
$70
特價
乳豬飯
每合 55 元
雞翼
3隻
$20
乳鴿皇每隻
$55
金牌鹽焗雞
$80
每份10元
豬耳
每盆
15元

# CHAR SIU

## BBQ PORK

**Serves 4**
**Preparation time 10 minutes**
**Resting time 12 hour**
**Cooking time 1 hour**

3 pounds 5 ounces (1.5 kg) boneless pork shoulder
3 tablespoons honey
2 cups (400 g) rice
4 heads bok choy (pak choi)

**FOR THE MARINADE:**
¼ cup (50 g) packed (soft) brown sugar
2 teaspoons salt
1 ounce (30 g) red bean curd
2 cloves garlic
¼ cup (60 ml) oyster sauce
¼ cup (60 ml) light soy sauce
2 tablespoons hoisin sauce
2 tablespoons Shaoxing wine
2 teaspoons Chinese five-spice powder
2 tablespoons honey

**At a time when I was a vegetarian, I said to myself, "I may not be a vegetarian for the rest of my life, but one thing that's *certain* is that I'll never eat pork again." However, I hadn't taken into account the sweet, caramelized fragrance of Hong Kong *char siu*, which quickly made me reconsider my stance. I could never say no to a tender, juicy, melt-in-the-mouth piece of caramelized *char siu,* preferably enjoyed in the company of Davina not far from Canton Road, in Kowloon. *Char siu* wasn't always the delightful dish it is today. There was a time when pork was of poor quality, so it was heavily seasoned to mask its taste and sliced thinly to save money. It was only when restaurants started using better quality meat that this dish became popular. *(Ada)***

The previous day, mix all the marinade ingredients together in a bowl.

Cut the meat into 3 to 4 long strips of equal size. Prick the strips all over with a fork. Put them into a shallow dish and coat evenly with the marinade. Massage the marinade into the meat, then squeeze tightly and cover with plastic wrap (clingfilm)—you can also place the strips with the marinade in a zip-top freezer bag, mix well, and squeeze out all the air before sealing the bag. Marinate for 12 hours in the refrigerator.

On the actual day, take the meat out of the refrigerator 1 hour before cooking.

Preheat the oven to 410°F (210°C/Gas Mark 6).

Line an ovenproof dish with aluminum foil. Place a suitably sized rack inside. Arrange the pieces of marinated pork on the rack, then add a large glass of water to the bottom of the dish to keep the meat from drying out during cooking.

Mix the remaining marinade with the slightly warmed honey.

Roast the pork for 15 minutes, then turn it over and brush with the honey-marinade mixture. Repeat the operation 3 times.

Cook the noodles according to the package directions.

Rinse the bok choy heads and cook in boiling water for 7 minutes.

Divide the rice into 4 bowls, arrange the *char siu* and bok choy over the rice, and serve.

### NOTE

Your *char siu* will probably be a shade less red than what you see displayed in Hong Kong. We chose not to use food coloring for a more natural result.

# CRISPY PORK BELLY

**Serves 6**
**Preparation time 25 minutes**
**Resting time 12 to 48 minutes**
**Cooking time 2 hours**

3-pound 5-ounce (1.5-kg) piece boneless pork belly, with skin

1 teaspoon (5 g) kosher (coarse) salt

3½ tablespoons (50 ml) white vinegar

**FOR THE MARINADE:**

2½ teaspoons (10 g) Chinese five-spice powder

1½ teaspoons (10 g) honey

1 teaspoon (5 g) salt

2¼ teaspoons (5 g) pepper

2 tablespoons oyster sauce

**Almost everywhere you find *char siu* and roast goose, you will also find crispy pork belly. Crispy skin and juicy, aromatic flesh make for a dish that Hong Kongers line up for at lunchtime in front of their favorite restaurant. *(Ada)***

The previous day, or even two days earlier, bring 8½ cups (2 liters) of water to a boil in a pot. Add the pork belly, rind side down, and immediately reduce the heat to low. Let simmer for 30 minutes.

Drain, then use a needle to poke holes all over the skin. Carefully wipe the skin clean with paper towels (kitchen paper).

Sprinkle the skin with the salt and rub to coat evenly. Let rest for 15 minutes.

Mix all the marinade ingredients together in a bowl.

Cut deep slits into the meat side of the pork belly every ¾ to 1 inch (2 or 3 cm) without cutting all the way through (stop when you reach the skin). Spread the marinade on the meat side, first inside the crevices, then over the entire surface.

Lay the pork belly, skin side up, in an ovenproof dish that is, if possible, only slightly larger than the meat. Clean the surface of the skin by scraping with the back of a knife, then brush with some of the vinegar. Put the dish into the refrigerator, uncovered, and let rest at least overnight (the longer the better—ideally 48 hours).

On the actual day, preheat the oven to 400°F (200°C/Gas Mark 6).

Roast the pork belly for 1 hour to 1 hour 15 minutes, depending on the size of the meat.

Poke a few more holes in the skin and brush again with the remaining vinegar. Increase the oven temperature to 450°F (230°C/Gas Mark 8) and roast for another 15 minutes on the top rack.

Cut the meat into cubes with the rind and serve hot, rind side down.

# ROAST GOOSE

**Serves 4 to 6**
**Preparation time 30 minutes**
**Resting time 3 to 4 days**
**Cooking time 1 hour**

1 goose

**FOR THE SUGAR GLAZE:**

2 tablespoons sugar
¼ cup (60 ml) white vinegar

**FOR THE MARINADE:**

5 teaspoons sugar
2 teaspoons salt
1 teaspoon ground ginger
1 teaspoon white pepper
⅓ cup (100 g) chu hou (fermented soybean) paste
⅓ cup (100 g) hoisin sauce
¾ ounce (15 g) fermented tofu
¼ cup (20 g) fresh ginger slices
3 tablespoons (20 g) chopped scallion (spring onion)

**When I was young, my grandmother would always scold me if ever I left any skin from a roast goose on my plate. "That's the best part," she would say, "the actual proof of a chef's expertise." I understand this better today—it's a challenge to achieve a thin, crispy, and golden-brown skin while keeping the meat juicy and tender. *(Davina)***

Start by blanching the goose in simmering water for about 10 seconds to slightly cook the surface. Next, make the glaze by mixing the sugar and vinegar. Brush it evenly over the entire goose.

Make the marinade by mixing all the ingredients together, then smear the marinade throughout the inside of the goose. Refrigerate for 3 to 4 days to dry. (This step is the key to a crispy skin.)

Preheat the oven to 325°F (160°C/Gas Mark 3), then roast the goose for 30 minutes.

Increase the oven temperature to 350° (180°C/Gas Mark 4) and continue to roast for 30 minutes, until the goose is completely cooked and the skin is crispy and golden.

Serve piping hot, ideally with plum sauce.

# ZONGZI

## STICKY RICE DUMPLINGS WRAPPED IN BAMBOO LEAVES

**Makes 6**
**Preparation time 30 minutes**
**Resting time overnight**
**Cooking time 2 hours**

- 18 bamboo leaves
- 2½ cups (480 g) glutinous (sticky) rice
- 2 teaspoons salt
- 1 tablespoon chicken bouillon (stock) powder
- 2 tablespoons vegetable oil
- 1⅓ cups (270 g) dried mung beans
- ¾ ounce (20 g) dried shrimp
- 3 dried shiitake mushrooms
- 4¼ ounces (120 g) pork belly
- 6 salted egg yolks

**FOR THE MARINADE:**

- 1 tablespoon Shaoxing wine
- 2 teaspoons chicken bouillon (stock) powder
- 1 teaspoon light soy sauce
- ½ teaspoon Chinese five-spice powder
- ½ teaspoon salt
- ¼ teaspoon white pepper
- ½ teaspoon sugar

***Zongzi*, also known as sticky rice dumplings, are a delicacy traditionally eaten during the Dragon Boat Festival. When I was a kid, this festival was always a highlight of the year—not only was it a public holiday, but I would also get to experience the festivities firsthand. My mother would take me to Stanley to watch the dragon boat races (see page 101). The pulsating beat of the drums, the cheering of the crowd, and the sight of the boats cleaving the water was a sensory extravaganza to be enjoyed by young and old alike. This recipe was shared with me by Éloise and her family, whom I would like to thank (see also page 94). *(Davina)***

The previous day, rinse the bamboo leaves thoroughly by hand to remove any impurities. Put the leaves into a large container, cover with water, and put a weight on top to keep them submerged. Let soak overnight.

Soak the rice in double the volume of water. Add 1 teaspoon of the salt, 1 teaspoon of the chicken bouillon powder, and 1 tablespoon of the oil. Cover and refrigerate overnight.

Do the same with the mung beans, adding the remaining 1 teaspoon of salt, 2 teaspoons of chicken bouillon powder, and 1 tablespoon of oil.

Rehydrate the dried shrimp and mushrooms separately by soaking them in water overnight.

Cut the pork belly into about ¾-ounce (20-g) pieces; each piece should contain a layer of meat and a layer of fat. Mix the pork with the marinade ingredients and coat well, then cover and refrigerate overnight.

On the actual day, drain all the soaked ingredients. Cut the mushrooms into quarters.

To make each dumpling, position a bamboo leaf staggered over another one with a two-thirds overlap. Carefully roll the leaves to form a cone, making sure there is no opening at the point. Fill the cone with 2 tablespoons of rice, 2 tablespoons of mung beans, ½ mushroom, 1 salted egg yolk, 1 teaspoon of shrimp, another 2 tablespoons of mung beans, and another 2 tablespoons of rice. Wrap a third leaf around the cone for stability, then fold over the top of the leaves to enclose the filling and form a tight pyramid. Tie the dumpling with kitchen string to secure.

Place the dumplings in a pot of water and bring to a boil over high heat. Reduce the heat to low, cover, and let cook for 2 hours.

Serve immediately. Unwrap and enjoy!

### NOTE

You can store any uncooked *zongzi* in an airtight container in the refrigerator for up to 3 days, or in the freezer for up to 1 month.

# NGONG PING AND VEGETARIAN CUISINE

## *DAVINA*

There's no denying that I'm a city girl. I love the energy of Hong Kong—the movement, the lights, the constant buzz. But that doesn't take away from the fact that I sometimes feel the need for calm. What I love most about this city is that, despite the never-ending hustle and bustle, there are also many havens of peace. This can sometimes mean throwing on a backpack and going for a hike in the mountains, gradually letting the city disappear behind me. And other times, it can also be something as simple as riding the Star Ferry—floating in the middle of Victoria Harbour, suspended between two shores, and a world away from the traffic, the crowds, and the hectic pace of everyday life.

The most underrated places to find peace and quiet are no doubt the temples. Although I'm not particularly religious, no matter how chaotic the city may seem, walking through the doors of a temple is like entering another world. The smell of burning incense fills the air; the murmur of prayers echoes in the background; and time seems to suddenly slow down.

Even so, despite all my years in Hong Kong, I had never visited the Po Lin Monastery, probably one of its most famous temples—that is, until 2019, when I took my boyfriend to Hong Kong for the first time and I finally discovered it. For once, I felt like a tourist in my hometown as we stood in wonder in front of the Big Buddha.

Unsurprisingly, the site attracts both tourists and devotees, some to admire the Buddha, others to study the scriptures and bronze statues that represent his past, present, and future lives. Hikers have not been overlooked—a mountain trail around Nei Lak Shan offers magnificent views of Lantau Peak and the South China Sea. Nevertheless, what intrigued me most was the monastery's vegetarian restaurant.

Unlike most Hong Kong restaurants, where imports make it possible to find practically every ingredient all year round, this one shows respect for the seasons. Meals are served according to the number of guests to avoid waste, and each dish showcases the best seasonal produce. Perhaps what struck me most was that there was a purpose to the food—there was as much philosophy as there was flavor—which came as a stark contrast to the abundance we often take for granted.

What intrigued me most
was the monastery's vegetarian restaurant.

# 港式檸檬茶

11 A.M. / 2 P.M.

# HONG KONG LEMON TEA

**Serves 3 to 4**
**Preparation time 15 minutes**

⅓ cup (30 g) Ceylon tea
¼ cup (20 g) orange pekoe tea
1 large lemon
Sugar or cane syrup

**Don't be fooled by its simplicity: Hong Kong lemon tea is much more than a simple lemon tea. Like its close cousin, milk tea (see page 32), it is a perfectly balanced drink in which the bold, earthy flavors of brewed tea mingle, in this case, with the acidic freshness of lemon. The iced version is what I like to order at a *cha chaan teng*, especially on sweltering summer days. There's something about that first icy sip—the way the acidity cuts through the bitterness of the tea—that makes it the perfect accompaniment to almost any meal. *(Davina)***

Follow the directions for preparing the tea base as described in the recipe for milk tea (see page 32).

Slice the lemon into thin rounds.

For hot lemon tea, fill a cup to halfway with the tea base. Add 2 to 3 lemon slices and top up with hot water. Using a spoon, gently crush the lemon slices to release their juice. Sweeten with sugar as desired and mix well.

For iced lemon tea, let the tea base cool, then refrigerate. Fill a glass to halfway with the tea base and add 2 to 3 lemon slices. Gently crush with a long spoon to release their juices. Add water and cane syrup as desired and mix well. Fill the glass with ice cubes and serve immediately.

12 PM / 3 PM →

# 下午茶

# YUM CHA
## *DAVINA*

Over the years, *yum cha* has gone beyond its role as the local equivalent of brunch to become a ritual that is deeply rooted in culture.

"Hey, call your grandma and ask her if she wants to do *yum cha* this Sunday."

*Yum cha*, literally "drinking tea," is an essential part of Cantonese food culture. Just as French families gather around their Sunday roast chicken and the British their traditional Sunday roast, Sunday in Hong Kong is often the occasion to do *yum cha*—in other words, to enjoy *dim sum* accompanied by Chinese tea.

The term *dim sum* refers to a wide variety of traditional small dishes, often served in bamboo steamer baskets. Among the most popular are *har gow*, a shrimp dumpling wrapped in a translucent pastry, and *siu mai*, a pork and shrimp dumpling wrapped in a thin yellow pastry. Another *dim sum* that is not to be missed, and probably my favorite, is *lor mai gai*, glutinous (sticky) rice topped with chicken, roasted meat, salted egg yolk, and mushrooms, all wrapped in a lotus leaf. When steamed, the lotus leaf releases its unique fragrance, impregnating the rice with a divine aroma.

Many of my childhood memories are of those Sunday *dim sum*, with the waiters pushing their carts stacked with steaming baskets as they shout out the names of the dishes, the smell of steam-heated bamboo mingling with the scent of freshly brewed tea—an utter feast for the senses for a child.

Growing up with this tradition, I also learned a few rules of *yum cha* etiquette that are passed down from generation to generation. One that has always amused me is that when someone serves you tea, instead of saying "thank you" out loud, you tap the table lightly with your index and middle fingers, as a sign of respect. My grandmother explained to me that this custom came from a Chinese legend linked to Emperor Qian Long, of the Qing dynasty. According to the legend, the emperor visited a teahouse in disguise, accompanied by his servants. When the emperor served them tea, his servants were unable to kowtow to him in reverence in the traditional Chinese way, so they discreetly tapped the table instead.

Over the years, *yum cha* has gone beyond its role as the local equivalent of brunch to become a ritual that is deeply rooted in culture. Much more than a meal, it is an occasion to share and to pass on tradition, connecting generations, friends, and loved ones.

# SIU MAI

## SHRIMP AND PORK STEAMED DUMPLINGS

**Makes 10**
**Preparation time 1 hour**
**Soaking time 2 hours**
**Refrigeration time 1 hour**
**Cooking time 10 minutes**

- 2 dried shiitake mushrooms
- 3½ ounces (100 g) raw shrimp (prawns), peeled
- 1¼ teaspoons salt
- ½ teaspoon baking soda (bicarbonate of soda)
- 3½ ounces (100 g) pork shoulder
- 4 teaspoons (15 g) lard (optional)
- 10 round wonton wrappers (square wrappers can also be cut to size)
- ¾ ounce (20 g) *tobiko* (flying fish roe)

**FOR THE SEASONING:**

- ½ teaspoon salt
- 1 teaspoon sugar
- ½ teaspoon chicken bouillon (stock) powder
- ¼ teaspoon white pepper
- ½ teaspoon light soy sauce
- 2½ teaspoons (10 g) lard
- 2 teaspoons sesame oil
- 1 tablespoon tapioca starch

**In my mind, *har gow* and *siu mai* are the undisputed kings of *dim sum*. No matter how many sophisticated new creations appear on the menu, these two classics are always popular. Every time a *dim sum* cart rolls out of the kitchen, the air is filled with steam and the unmistakable aroma of freshly cooked dumplings, and I sit up straight and wait for the servers to shout out the magic words: "*har gow, siu mai!*" That's my cue. I leap from my chair and weave my way between the tables, dodging other impatient diners, and triumphantly return with a bamboo steamer basket filled with *siu mai*. *(Davina)***

Rehydrate the mushrooms by soaking them in water for 2 hours. When softened, squeeze out the excess water, cut off the tough stems (stalks), and mince (very finely cut).

Mix the shrimp with ¼ teaspoon of the salt and ¼ teaspoon of the baking soda. Marinate for 15 minutes, then rinse thoroughly under running water. Pat dry and cut into small pieces.

Cut the pork into small pieces, then rinse, drain, and dry. Finely chop the lard, if using, and add to the shrimp and salt.

Sprinkle the pork with the remaining ¼ teaspoon of baking soda and with ½ teaspoon of water, then mix well. Add the shrimp and the remaining 1 teaspoon of salt (with the lard, if using), then mix vigorously in one direction with a pair of chopsticks until the ingredients are completely combined and the filling forms a sticky paste.

Incorporate the seasoning ingredients and chopped mushrooms. Mix well, then cover and refrigerate for 1 hour.

Line a bamboo steamer basket with perforated parchment (baking) paper (perforated parchment paper disks to fit bamboo steamers are available at Asian grocery stores).

Place 1 tablespoon of the filling on a wonton wrapper. Pinch the sides of the wrapper together to create a pouch. Continue to add filling until it sticks out a little from the pouch. Flatten the surface and cover with the *tobiko*.

Repeat the operation until the ingredients are all used, then arrange the dumplings in the steamer. Steam for 10 minutes over high heat and serve immediately.

# HAR GOW

## STEAMED SHRIMP DUMPLINGS

**Makes 10**
**Preparation time 45 minutes**
**Soaking time 15 minutes**
**Resting time 15 minutes**
**Cooking time 6 minutes**

**FOR THE FILLING:**

4 ounces (110 g) raw shrimp (prawns), peeled

¼ teaspoon salt

¼ teaspoon baking soda (bicarbonate of soda)

2 tablespoons (15 g) bamboo shoots

4 teaspoons (15 g) lard (optional)

**FOR THE SEASONING:**

¼ teaspoon salt

½ teaspoon sugar

⅛ teaspoon white pepper

½ teaspoon Shaoxing wine

1½ teaspoons egg white

½ teaspoon sesame oil

1 teaspoon cornstarch (bicarbonate of soda)

**FOR THE WRAPPERS:**

⅓ cup (40 g) wheat starch

⅓ cup (40 g) tapioca starch (flour; or cornstarch/cornflour)

1½ teaspoons lard (or vegetable oil)

**The one type of *dim sum* that everybody knows has to be *har gow*. To my amazement, you even find it served as an appetizer in many Asian restaurants in Paris, even those that aren't strictly Cantonese. However, I hardly ever order them in France. Although these dumplings may look simple enough, it's rare to find really good ones.**

Cut the shrimp into small pieces and put them in a bowl with the salt and baking soda. Marinate for 15 minutes.

Finely chop the bamboo shoots and cut the lard into dice.

Add the seasoning ingredients to the shrimp and mix vigorously until the mixture has a slightly sticky consistency. Add the bamboo shoots and lard and mix until combined, then cover the bowl and refrigerate.

To make the dough for the wrappers, add ⅓ cup (85 ml) of boiling water to a bowl with the wheat starch and mix vigorously to a smooth dough. Let rest for 5 minutes.

Lightly flatten the dough and sprinkle with half the tapioca starch, then knead to incorporate. Repeat with the remaining tapioca starch until the dough is smooth and pliable. Incorporate the lard and continue to knead for a few minutes. Cover and let rest for 10 minutes.

Roll the dough into a long log and divide into ten pieces, weighing about ⅜ ounce (10 g) each. Roll each piece into a ball and flatten slightly. Oil a rolling pin and the work surface, then roll out each ball into a disk about 2 inches (5 cm) in diameter, with the edges thinner than the center.

Place 1 teaspoon of filling in the center of a wrapper. Pleat one side of the disk, forming 8 to 10 pleats from one end of the side to the other and leaving the other side smooth. Pinch the sides together to seal the dumpling, keeping its slightly curved shape. Repeat the process until all the ingredients are completely used.

Arrange the dumplings in a bamboo steamer basket lined with perforated parchment (baking) paper (perforated parchment paper disks to fit bamboo steamers are available at Asian grocery stores) and steam for 5 to 6 minutes. Serve immediately.

# CHAR SIU BAO

## STEAMED BBQ PORK BUNS

**Makes 12**
**Preparation time 40 minutes**
**Resting time 36 hours plus 2 hours**
**Cooking time 30 minutes**

**FOR THE STARTER (*LAOMIAN*):**

½ small cake (11 g) fresh yeast or 1½ teaspoons active dry (fast-action dried) yeast

1⅔ cups (200 g) cake (Italian '00') flour

**FOR THE FILLING:**

2 scallions (spring onions)

1 tablespoon vegetable oil

1 tablespoon light soy sauce

1 tablespoon dark soy sauce

1 tablespoon hoisin sauce

1 tablespoon sesame oil

1 teaspoon packed (soft) brown sugar

1 tablespoon cornstarch (cornflour)

3½ ounces (100 g) *char siu* (see page 68)

**FOR THE DOUGH:**

⅔ cup (130 g) sugar

4 teaspoons (20 g) unsalted butter, softened

8 drops alkaline water

1¼ cups (150 g) cake (Italian '00') flour

⅝ teaspoon (2 g) ammonium carbonate (baker's ammonia)

3¾ teaspoons baking powder

**Although bao may not have been part of my childhood, the feeling I get from biting into one of these fluffy buns while it's still too hot and the dough sticks to my teeth is like what Proust experienced with his madeleine. You can tell a perfect *char siu bao* by how the top of the bun cracks open as it steams. It is even said that this opening brings good luck to certain restaurants, and that the more the buns open, the more customers will flock to them.**

Two days in advance, prepare the starter by mixing the yeast with 2 tablespoons (30 ml) of lukewarm water and ⅓ cup plus 1 tablespoon (50 g) of flour. Cover and let stand overnight at room temperature.

The next day, refresh the starter with ⅓ cup plus 1 tablespoon (50 g) of flour and 2 tablespoons (30 ml) of water. Cover and let stand for another 12 hours.

The following day, add ⅔ cup plus 2 tablespoons (100 g) of flour and ¼ cup (60 ml) of water, then let stand overnight. The starter should have doubled in volume and be soft, a little sticky, and smelling of alcohol.

To make the filling, wash and chop the white scallion bulbs. Put a saucepan with the other ingredients (except the cornstarch and *char siu*) over low heat until the sugar melts, stirring regularly. Incorporate the cornstarch to thicken the mixture. Add the *char siu*, cut into small cubes. Continue to cook for another 5 minutes and set aside.

To make the dough, mix the starter with the sugar and very soft butter in a stand mixer fitted with a flat paddle beater for 3 minutes, then add the alkaline water. Incorporate the flour, ammonium carbonate, and baking powder, then knead for another 5 minutes in the mixer. Finish kneading by hand until the dough is smooth. Transfer the dough to a bowl, cover with a cloth, and let rest for 2 hours at room temperature.

Roll the dough into a log and divide into 12 pieces. Roll out each piece of dough into a disk, with the edges thinner than the center.

Place 1 heaping spoonful of filling in the center of a dough disk and pleat the top to close the bun. Repeat the process until all the ingredients are completely used. Place the buns in a bamboo steamer over a pot of boiling water. Steam the buns over high heat (the water should boil) for 15 to 20 minutes, depending on their size.

### NOTE

It is important to steam the buns over high heat. This helps them to crack open as they cook, because they are forced to plump up quickly.

信箱在後面

# XIAO LONG BAO

## SOUP DUMPLINGS

**Makes 15**
**Preparation time 30 minutes**
**Cooking time 2 hours plus 10 minutes**
**Resting time overnight plus 30 minutes**

**FOR THE BROTH:**

2¼ pounds (1 kg) chicken bones (wings, legs), skin on

1 bunch scallions (spring onions)

2-inch (5-cm) length fresh ginger

1 tablespoon white pepper

1 tablespoon salt

**FOR THE WRAPPERS:**

2 cups (250 g) cake (Italian '00') flour

1 pinch salt

**FOR THE FILLING:**

8¾ ounces (250 g) ground (minced) pork

2 tablespoons light soy sauce

1 tablespoon Shaoxing wine

2 tablespoons packed (soft) brown sugar

**Although "little dragon" dumplings aren't native to Hong Kong (they come from the Shanghai region of China), they can still be found on the menu of many *dim sum* restaurants. These delectable dumplings are shrouded with an air of mystery. How do they put the soup inside? How do they get the wrapper to be so delicate? How do you eat them without risking third-degree burns? *(Ada)***

The previous day, make the broth (stock) by putting all the ingredients into a pot and adding 8½ cups (2 liters) of water. Bring to a simmer and let cook, uncovered, for 2 hours. Strain the broth and refrigerate overnight.

On the actual day, make the wrappers. Mix the flour with the salt. Gradually incorporate scant 1 cup (220 ml) of warm water to form a dough. Depending on the flour you use, you may need more or less water, so don't add it all at once. Knead vigorously until the dough is smooth. Cover with a damp cloth and let rest for 30 minutes.

Mix all the filling ingredients to a smooth paste. Add about 3½ tablespoons (50 ml) of the now gelatinous chicken broth and whisk to combine. Refrigerate until ready to use.

To shape the wrappers, take a few small pieces of dough at a time, about ⅛ ounce (5 g), and roll out into disks. Cover the dough with a cloth or plastic wrap (clingfilm) between rolling operations to keep them from drying out.

Place 1 tablespoon filling in the center of a wrapper (about ⅝ ounce/ 18 g). Pleat the top of the dumpling to seal. Repeat the process until all the ingredients are completely used.

Arrange the dumplings in a bamboo steamer basket lined with perforated parchment (baking) paper (perforated parchment paper disks to fit bamboo steamers are available at Asian grocery stores) and steam for 10 minutes.

## HOW TO EAT

They are usually eaten with a Chinese soup spoon, which have deeper sides than a normal spoon. There are several techniques:

- If you're impatient, you can gulp it down all at once and burn yourself.
- If you're impatient, you can pierce a hole in the dumpling with a chopstick, let the soup run into the spoon, then slurp up the soup before biting into the dumpling.
- If you're patient, you can wait a few minutes before eating it whole in a single mouthful.

At Din Tai Fung, *xiao long bao* are served with a small bowl of fresh ginger cut into matchsticks, over which you pour soy sauce and black rice vinegar.

## NOTE

For this recipe, it is impossible to cheat by using chicken bouillon (stock) cubes. Bones are needed to release collagen, which enables the broth to solidify so that it can melt when the dumplings are steamed.

# LOR MAI GAI

## LOTUS-WRAPPED GLUTINOUS RICE WITH CHICKEN

**Serves 2**
**Preparation time 45 minutes**
**Soaking time 50 minutes**
**Cooking time 1 hour**
**Resting time 15 minutes**

**You'll know that you've become a true lover of Hong Kong food if you get as excited about unwrapping a *lor mai gai* as you do about opening a Christmas present. You'll feel the same sense of anticipation as you carefully spread apart the lotus leaves to reveal the treasures hidden inside—with each one being different, depending on where you are. *(Davina)***

1 dried lotus leaf
2 dried shiitake mushrooms
1⅓ cups (250 g) glutinous (sticky) rice
½ teaspoon salt
1 shallot
5¼ ounces (150 g) boneless chicken leg (about 1 leg)
½ teaspoon cornstarch (cornflour)
2 salted egg yolks
1 Chinese sausage (*lap cheong*)
Vegetable oil

**FOR THE SAUCE:**

¼ teaspoon light soy sauce
⅜ teaspoon dark soy sauce
¼ teaspoon oyster sauce
⅛ teaspoon Shaoxing wine
¼ teaspoon sugar
⅛ teaspoon salt
⅛ teaspoon white pepper
¼ teaspoon sesame oil

Soak the lotus leaf in a large container filled with water for 30 minutes. Weigh it down with a heavy object, such as a plate, to make sure it remains completely submerged. Once the leaf is pliable, drain off the water. Next, pour over boiling water and let soak for 5 minutes to remove any bitterness. Drain the leaf again and rinse under cold water. Cut into quarters and remove the hard central stem. Rehydrate the mushrooms by soaking in cold water for 15 minutes, then cut in half.

Rinse the rice thoroughly under running water, then drain. Lightly oil a deep heatproof dish and spread the rice in an even layer.

Mix the salt with 1 tablespoon of oil and 1 cup (250 ml) water. Pour the mixture over the rice and stir gently to let the rice absorb the liquid, which should just cover the surface. Level the rice for even cooking and cook in a steamer for 20 to 25 minutes over high heat.

Thinly slice the shallot. Cut the chicken into small cubes and mix with the cornstarch and 1 teaspoon of water. Cut the salted egg yolks in half. Cut the sausage into 8 equal pieces.

Place the mushrooms, egg yolks, and sausage pieces on top of the rice and cook for another 15 minutes. Let rest for 15 minutes.

Mix all the sauce ingredients together.

Heat 2 tablespoons of oil in a wok over high heat until lightly smoking, then reduce the heat to medium. Sauté the shallot until fragrant and golden. Add the chicken and sauce, then stir continuously until the chicken is completely cooked. Remove from the heat.

Place a lotus leaf quarter on top of another so that only the wider parts are overlapping. The narrower ends should be pointing left and right. Brush with oil.

Place about ⅔ cup (125 g) rice in the center, flattening it slightly to create a small well. Spread 1 tablespoon chicken filling inside the well and then arrange 1 mushroom, 1 salted egg yolk, and 4 sausage pieces in the center. Add about ⅔ cup (125 g) more rice, flattening to completely cover the filling.

Fold the corners of the lotus leaf toward the center, starting with the bottom, followed by the top. Fold over the left side and then the right to completely wrap the rice to form a square bundle. Turn over and press gently to keep them from unfolding, then wrap the bundle in parchment (baking) paper. Repeat the process until all the ingredients are completely used and steam the bundles for 10 minutes.

If you store the freshly wrapped bundles in the refrigerator, steam them 25 minutes before serving.

Unwrap and serve hot.

### NOTE

Freshly wrapped bundles can be stored in an airtight container for up to 3 days in the refrigerator. They will also keep for up to 1 month in the freezer. In that case, steam from frozen for 30 to 35 minutes.

# LO BAK GO

## TURNIP CAKE

**Serves 3 to 4**
**Preparation time 1 hour**
**Soaking time 1 hour**
**Cooking time 1 hour 10 minutes**

⅓ cup (15 g) dried shrimp
2 dried shiitake mushrooms
2 Chinese sausages (*lap cheong*)
1¼ pounds (550 g) daikon (mooli) radish
½ teaspoon salt
1 teaspoon chicken bouillon (stock) powder
⅓ block (about 1 ounce/25 g) Chinese brown sugar
Vegetable oil

**FOR THE BATTER:**
1 cup (140 g) rice flour (ground rice)
3½ tablespoons (25 g) cornstarch (cornstarch)
3½ tablespoons (25 g) wheat starch (optional, to improve texture; omit for a gluten-free version)
1 teaspoon salt
1 tablespoon chicken bouillon (stock) powder
½ teaspoon white pepper
1 tablespoon vegetable oil

***Lo bak*** **is the Cantonese word for the Japanese daikon radish, which resembles a turnip but has a milder and sweeter flavor. Although, confusingly, *lo bak go* is translated into English as turnip cake, it is actually made with this radish, which gives the cake its characteristic texture and flavor. My thanks to Éloise for her recipe. *(Davina)***

Rinse the dried shrimp and mushrooms before soaking them in water for 1 hour to rehydrate. Drain, collecting the soaking water, and cut both into ¼-inch (5-mm) dice. Cut the sausages into ¼-inch (5-mm) dice.

Heat 1 tablespoon of oil in a skillet (frying pan) over medium heat and sauté the mushrooms, shrimp, and sausages for 3 minutes, until fragrant. The sausages should be cooked through.

Peel the radish and cut into 1/16-inch (2-mm)-thick slices, then into 2¾ by ¼-inch (7 cm × 5-mm) matchsticks, or shred.

Heat 1 tablespoon oil in a skillet over medium heat and sauté the radish with the salt and chicken bouillon powder, stirring to combine. Add 1¼ cups (300 ml) of water and the sugar. Cover and bring to a boil over medium heat. Reduce the heat to low and cook for 8 to 10 minutes, stirring occasionally to keep it from burning. When completely cooked, the radish should be tender with only a thin layer of water remaining. Remove from the heat.

To make the batter, mix together the rice flour, cornstarch and wheat starch. Incorporate the salt, chicken bouillon powder, pepper, and scant 1 cup (200 ml) shrimp and mushroom soaking water to form a smooth batter. Add the oil and mix to incorporate.

Add one-quarter of this batter to the still-warm radish mixture and mix well, then stir in the rest until smooth. Incorporate two-thirds of the mushroom, shrimp, and sausage mixture.

Grease a 7-inch (18-cm)-diameter round baking pan with oil and fill with the batter. Sprinkle with the remaining mushroom mixture. Cover with aluminum foil, leaving a slight opening at the sides to let steam circulate, and cook in a steamer over medium heat for 1 hour. Check for doneness by inserting a chopstick or toothpick (cocktail stick) into the center: it should come out clean.

Let cool to room temperature, then cover and refrigerate. To reheat before serving, steam the turnip cake, or pan-fry for a crispy texture.

12 P.M. / 3 P.M.

# CHEUNG FUN

## STEAMED SHRIMP RICE NOODLE ROLLS

**No *dim sum* meal is complete for me without ordering a steaming hot plate of soft *cheung fun* filled with shrimp, my favorite. The best can be found at Lin Heung Tea House. I love to sit down after grabbing a few steamer baskets from a cart, and then wait until the cart I want passes close to my table. When the server hands me my plate after drizzling it with plenty of sauce, no matter what there might be on the table at the time, the *cheung fun* is the first one I'll devour. *(Ada)***

**Serves 4**
**Preparation time 20 minutes**
**Resting time 40 minutes**
**Cooking time 30 minutes**

14 ounces (400 g) raw shrimp (prawns)
1 teaspoon salt
1 teaspoon white pepper
1 teaspoon cornstarch (cornflour)
Vegetable oil

**FOR THE SAUCE:**

½-inch (1-cm) length fresh ginger
2 scallions (spring onions)
3 teaspoons light soy sauce
2 teaspoons packed (soft) brown sugar
1 tablespoon dark soy sauce
1 tablespoon oyster sauce
1 tablespoon vegetable oil

**FOR THE NOODLES:**

¼ cup (40 g) rice flour (ground flour)
1½ tablespoons (10 g) mung bean/chickpea (besan/gram) flour
¼ cup (30 g) cornstarch (cornflour)
1 teaspoon salt

Make the sauce. Peel and finely slice the ginger. Chop the white scallion bulbs.

In a pan, mix all the sauce ingredients with 3 tablespoons of water. Put it over low heat for 5 minutes, then let cool. Strain to remove the ginger and scallions.

To make the noodle batter, mix the flours with the starch and salt. Gradually stir in about 1 cup (230 ml) of hot water until combined. The batter should be runny. Let stand for about 40 minutes.

Peel and halve the shrimp. Mix together the salt, pepper, and cornstarch, then dredge the shrimp in the mixture. Let stand for 10 minutes, then steam for 5 minutes.

To make the rice noodle sheets, you will need a flat container with deep sides. I use a small, deep sheet pan. If your steamer isn't large enough for it to fit inside, you can use a large skillet (frying pan) or wok. You need to be able to fit your container inside and cover everything with a lid.

Bring water to a boil in the steamer (or wok or skillet).

Grease the container with oil. Add 1 ladle of batter to the container and place it inside the steamer. Steam for 3 minutes. Arrange 3 shrimp in a line on the noodle wrapper, cook for another 1 minute, and then wrap into a roll. Repeat the process until all the ingredients are completely used, then serve with the sauce.

### NOTE

Remember to mix the batter well before each use; the flours quickly sink to the bottom.

### VARIATIONS

You can fill your *cheung fun* with anything you want, including *char siu*, ground (minced) beef, scallions, and dried shrimp. Why not create your own? You can also add aromatics and condiments of your choice, such as scallions, sesame seeds, and sriracha sauce.

# CRISPY SHRIMP WONTONS

**Makes 8**
**Preparation time 10 minutes**
**Marinating time 30 minutes**
**Cooking time 3 minutes**

½-inch (1-cm) length fresh ginger
1 scallion (spring onion)
2 tablespoons light soy sauce
8 raw shrimp (prawns), peeled
1 tablespoon cornstarch (cornflour)
8 wonton wrappers
Vegetable oil

**Crispy wontons are among my favorite dumplings. The best I've ever tried were in Sai Kung, where I went one morning with my brother before going on a hike. We were waiting for our boat when we saw all these *dim sum* and fish restaurants along the waterfront, and, although we had no real reason to sit down, we just did. this was a good thing, because the crispy shrimp wontons we had there were the best in the world—yes, in the world! *(Ada)***

Peel and chop the ginger. Chop the scallions.

Mix the ginger and scallions with the soy sauce and 1 tablespoon of oil. Marinate the shrimp in the mixture for 30 minutes, then drain and dredge in the cornstarch.

On a floured work surface, roll out the wonton wrappers to make them even thinner. Place a shrimp on the bottom half of a wrapper. Fold the top half over and seal the edges and corners. Fold again by bringing two corners together and pressing.

Heat 2 cups (500 ml) of oil in a pot or deep fryer (if using a pot, be careful not to let the oil burn). When the oil is hot (you can test the temperature by tossing in a few breadcrumbs, which should brown), deep-fry the wontons for 2 to 3 minutes.

Serve hot and eat quickly; be careful not to burn your tongue.

# STANLEY, TAI TAM, THE TWINS
## *ADA*

Hong Kong has a reputation—and rightly so—for being a city of luxury, a flashy place where everything sparkles.

However, I always find that the most unsuspected luxury there is the ability to take a bus for a few stops and alight in a nature park, at a reservoir, or at the foot of a mountain and suddenly hear nothing but birds and running water.

Stanley, a town at the southern end of Hong Kong Island, is basically a collection of fairly luxurious residential districts—which are a magnet for expatriates, including many French people—and a market, but most of all, it's a magical place to enjoy nature, one that makes you feel as though you're on a trip far away from Hong Kong.

I discovered the Tai Tam Reservoir in Stanley during the loveliest time of the year: November. The sun was shining and it was early, maybe seven o'clock in the morning. I was filled with childlike wonder as I could see through the tree branches the leafy hills that overlook this expanse of turquoise water, which I would cross many times by bus.

It quickly became a morning ritual for me to take minibus number 16 and get off at the reservoir, and then to walk or run along the path, listening to nothing but my sneakers on the concrete, the branches crackling under the feet of a bird (or a wild boar), the waterfall below, or the sparrows telling each other about their lives—wow, they sure have a lot to talk about! On weekdays, I would also come across a lot of older people walking briskly along the street, with a radio in their pocket playing Chinese pop music.

There are so many different routes you can take that start from the Tai Tam Reservoir. Simply walking around the reservoir takes no more than an hour. More stamina and ambition is needed to hike all the way to Quarry Bay, a financial district in the northeast of the island, which is reached by crossing a mountainous stretch. The beach at Repulse Bay can also be reached on a one-hour walk along a catchwater. Catchwaters are large (sometimes very large) concrete gutters that collect the water from heavy rains (black rainstorms[12] and typhoons, in particular) and prevent landslides.

12. The highest level of rainstorm in Hong Kong.

As the name suggests, The Twins, also known as Twin Peaks, are two mountains standing side by side. You can start your hike (which is what I always do) just north of Stanley. Section 1 of the Wilson Trail, also known as The Twins Hike, has the reputation of being one of the toughest trails in Hong Kong. I would describe it as an opportunity to explore your relationship with your calves. It begins with a seemingly endless flight of steps (several sections take you up or down 400 steps, and the descent is even less pleasant than the climb).

But you are rewarded with a boost to your self-esteem, extraordinary views over Stanley and Stanley Bay, and the stretches of peaceful, remote, and exotic mountain and forest scenery. The walk continues over Violet Hill, and back into the city through the Tai Hang district (see page 58), just above Happy Valley.

There is a clean, easily accessible, and family-friendly beach at Stanley that is the starting point for dragon boat[13] and windsurf races. However, it isn't Turtle Cove, which is farther away. You can catch a glimpse of it from the number 16 or 14 bus as they pass right by the Tai Tam reservoir.

13. A kind of dugout canoe with a dragon's head.

People bring charcoal and grill racks to these places and spend the afternoon or evening around a barbecue.

This tiny cove is set below the cliff at the foot of Red Hill Peninsula, an upmarket residential complex. The beach here has clear water and fine sand, and nearby are concrete barbecue tables that are also features found at other beaches, promenades, and parks. People bring charcoal and grill racks to these places and spend the afternoon or evening around a barbecue. I've always found this beach to be a little crowded. The last time I swam there was in December. As I was swimming, I came across a gentleman in his sixties who asked me what I was doing here on a weekday morning, if I lived in Hong Kong, and why I liked this city so much. I pointed to everything around me, and replied: "Look, sir, and it's December." He laughed and told me that was why he had never left.

# 奶黃包
# STEAMED CUSTARD BUNS

**Makes 8**
**Preparation time 20 minutes**
Resting time **1 hour 20 minutes**
**Cooking time 15 minutes**

**FOR THE DOUGH:**

4 teaspoons active dry (fast-action dried) yeast

1⅓ cups (170 g) all-purpose (plain) flour

1 pinch salt

1 tablespoon (10 g) sugar

**FOR THE CUSTARD FILLING:**

4 eggs

3½ tablespoons (50 g) salted butter, softened

⅓ cup (40 g) confectioners' (icing) sugar

3½ tablespoons (50 ml) whole (full-fat) milk

¼ cup (30 g) cornstarch (cornflour)

**It's a custom of mine to eat these buns in the streets of Wan Chai, amid the market stalls. The soft texture of the fluffy bun and the warmth it radiates as it comes fresh out of the steamer remind me of my little sister's plump cheeks, and I find the sweet, yet savory taste of the custard comforting. When I make these at home, I often make eight and freeze seven, so that I can eat them whenever I want. *(Ada)***

To make the dough, dissolve the yeast in 6 tablespoons (90 ml) of lukewarm water and let stand for 5 minutes.

Put the flour and salt into a stand mixer. Run the mixer and add the sugar, followed by the water and yeast to form a dough. Knead well for about 5 minutes, until the dough is perfectly smooth. Cover with a damp cloth and let rise for 1 hour.

To make the filling, hard-boil 3 eggs for 9 minutes. Beat the last egg in a bowl.

Shell the hard-boiled eggs, separate the whites from the yolks, and finely crush the yolks with a fork. Add the butter and sugar and mix with a spatula, then with a handheld mixer. While beating, add the lukewarm milk, then sift in the cornstarch. Incorporate the beaten egg and continue to beat.

Transfer the mixture to a saucepan and place over low heat, beating vigorously and continuously until the custard thickens.

When the dough has risen, gather into a ball and divide into 8 pieces. Roll out each dough ball into a disk, with the edges thinner than the center. Place 1 spoonful of filling in the middle, encase in the dough, and shape into a smooth ball. Place the bun in a steamer basket lined with perforated parchment (baking) paper (perforated parchment paper disks to fit bamboo steamers are available at Asian grocery stores), smooth side up. Repeat the process until all ingredients are completely used, then steam over medium heat for 7 minutes.

Wait a few minutes before lifting the lid. Serve warm.

# BRAISED CHICKEN FEET WITH BLACK BEAN SAUCE

**Serves 4**
**Preparation time 30 minutes**
**Refrigeration time 1 hour**
**Cooking time 1 hour 10 minutes**

1 pound 2 ounces (500 g) chicken feet
1 tablespoon Shaoxing wine
1 tablespoon rice vinegar
1 scallion (spring onion)
1 tablespoon honey (or maltose)
scant 1½ cups (340 ml) vegetable oil
6 slices ginger
3 cloves garlic
1 large (30 g) shallot
3 red chiles
2 star anise
2 tablespoons (30 g) fermented black beans
⅛ small (10 g) red bell pepper (optional, for garnish)

**FOR THE SAUCE:**

1 tablespoon black bean sauce
2 tablespoons oyster sauce
1 tablespoon light soy sauce
1 tablespoon dark soy sauce
1 tablespoon Shaoxing wine
2 tablespoons sugar
1 teaspoon salt
1 tablespoon hoisin sauce
½ teaspoon red bean paste
1 tablespoon chili sauce (optional)

**I can't help smiling at the way some people react when I mention to them that I love to eat chicken feet. This dish is so common In Hong Kong that most children learn how to eat it at the same time as they learn how to use chopsticks.** ***(Davina)***

Place the chicken feet in a saucepan of cold water and add the Shaoxing wine, vinegar, scallion, cut into 1¼-inch (4-cm) lengths, and honey. Bring to a boil, then reduce the heat and let cook for 3 minutes.

Drain, then thoroughly pat the feet dry to prevent oil splatter when deep-frying. Cut each foot in half and remove the claws.

Heat the oil in a wok to 350°F (180°C). Add the feet and cover with a lid to reduce any splatter. After 2 to 3 minutes, turn the feet to make sure they fry evenly. Deep-fry until beautifully golden, then remove from the oil. Set aside some of the oil.

Immediately shock the feet by submerging them into a large bowl of ice water. This will produce the wrinkly surface texture known as "tiger skin." Refrigerate for 1 hour.

To make the sauce, mix the black bean sauce, oyster sauce, soy sauces, Shaoxing wine, sugar, salt, hoisin sauce, and red bean paste. Add the chili sauce, if using.

Heat 1 tablespoon of oil in a wok and fry the ginger for 30 seconds, then add the garlic, shallots, and chopped chiles. Add the star anise and fermented beans, followed by the sauce, and stir-fry for 1 minute.

Add the chicken feet and coat well with the sauce. Cover the contents of the wok with hot water and bring to a boil. Reduce the heat to medium, cover, and simmer for 40 minutes.

Arrange the braised chicken feet in a bowl (garnish with slices of red bell pepper and/or fermented black beans, if using), put into a large wok or steamer, and steam for 12 minutes before serving.

# SESAME BALLS

**After a long time believing that sesame balls would be difficult to make, I was surprised to learn that the recipe requires only a few simple ingredients. My mother never let me make them at home, which I attributed to them being too complicated. I now realize it was because she knew how tempted I would be to eat them straight out of the frying oil.** ***(Davina)***

**Makes 8**
**Preparation time 15 minutes**
**Cooking time 20 minutes**

⅓ cup plus 1 tablespoon (80 g) sugar
1¼ cups (200 g) glutinous rice flour (ground sticky rice)
White sesame seeds
Vegetable oil

Make a syrup by dissolving sugar in a small saucepan in ½ cup (125 ml) of water, stirring continuously.

Put the flour into a large bowl and gradually stir in the hot syrup. When a smooth dough forms, add 1 teaspoon of oil and knead to a smooth and firm ball.

Divide the dough into 8 equal pieces and roll each piece into a ball. Lightly moisten the surface, then roll in sesame seeds until completely covered.

Heat 4¼ cups (1 liter) oil to 265°F (130°C) in a large saucepan. Carefully dip the sesame balls into the oil and deep-fry over medium-low heat, turning continuously, for about 10 minutes. Using a skimmer, gently press the balls against the sides to encourage expansion.

When the sesame balls rise to the surface, increase the oil temperature to 320°F (160°C) and continue to cook for about 5 minutes, until golden brown. Drain on paper towels (kitchen paper) and serve piping hot.

## NOTE

Sesame balls are best eaten on the same day; they can lose their crunch over time.

# 楊枝甘露

# MANGO POMELO SAGO SOUP

**Serves 4**
**Preparation time 15 minutes**
**Resting time 2 hours**
**Cooking time 10 minutes**

⅔ cup (100 g) tapioca pearls

2 ripe mangoes

¾ cup (175 ml) unsweetened coconut cream

1 pomelo

**This dessert is a favorite among Hong Kong locals, and it is often served from the carts in *dim sum* restaurants. It is usually served chilled, especially on hot days. In my case, I make a batch for serving four people, put it into small jars, and store in the refrigerator. That way I can eat it all week long. I love the sweetness of this dessert, its smooth texture, and the small pieces of pomelo pulp that click under the tongue. *(Ada)***

Cook the tapioca over low heat with scant 1 cup (200 ml) water, stirring regularly.

Peel the mangoes. Blend the flesh of 1 mango with the coconut cream. Dice the second.

Peel the pomelo and separate the flesh into small pieces.

Add the tapioca to the mango-and-coconut mixture and stir well to separate the pearls. Finally, add the pomelo pieces and stir gently to prevent crushing. Refrigerate for at least 2 hours.

Serve with fresh mango dice.

# TRANSPORTATION IN HONG KONG
## *ADA*

Hong Kong has a lot going for it, a long list that includes tropical landscapes, butterflies by the thousands, a breathtaking skyline, lush forests, and an exceptional food scene. But what really appealed to me and made me want to live there was the transportation system.

I live in Paris. I've been using the Metro subway trains every day for many, many years. Has there ever been a day without *any* transportation problems? Yes, but not in Paris—this is in Hong Kong. The Mass Transit Railway, or MTR, is modern, efficient, fast, punctual, clean, and goes practically everywhere. The airport is only a 15-minute ride from Central, and Kowloon and the New Territories are within easy reach. Another bonus is that the exits are well designed and perfectly signposted.

As if the MTR wasn't efficient enough, the city has a network of buses, often double-decker, that zip along the main streets as fast as they do over mountain passes. I love them because they're a great way to see the city, especially when it's hot. I often take the bus from the beginning of the line, at Stanley, and sit upstairs at the front. I sometimes flinch when heavy tree branches whip across the front window, but I can take in the view over the whole of Stanley Bay, then the beaches of Repulse Bay and Deep Water Bay, before going through the tunnel under the mountain and reappearing either near Wan Chai or Happy Valley, and suddenly we're downtown.

I love the minibuses, too. There are two types: green and red. They often have 16 or 19 seats, and the driver never allows more people to board than there are seats.

As if the MTR wasn't efficient enough, the city has a network of buses.

The green minibuses are publicly operated and are just like the normal city buses, with a fixed fare and route. The red minibuses are privately owned, with varying fares announced by the driver at the entrance, but they can stop just about anywhere. The red minibuses are more like a form of ride-sharing. It's in the driver's interest to go fast, so journeys can be chaotic. Whether you are waiting at a stop for a red or green minibus, you may find that the driver doesn't stop for you. Sometimes it's because the bus is full. Sometimes, we just don't know.

Linking Hong Kong Island (from Wan Chai or Central) to Tsim Sha Tsui, the Star Ferry is so emblematic of Hong Kong that it features on everything from magnets, stickers, and coloring books to T-shirts and caps. Before boarding, you have to decide whether you want to travel on the upper deck or the lower deck. Once you embark, no change is possible. The reversible backrests on the Star Ferry's wooden benches is a most ingenious invention, allowing you to change which way you face, depending on the direction of the journey. In fact, the Star Ferry operates in both directions without turning around—an ingenious idea.

Finally, taxicabs are a popular method of transportation in Hong Kong, particularly for people who aren't eager to descend to the depths of the huge MTR stations.

There are three colors: red, which is for taxicabs serving Hong Kong Island and Kowloon; green, for those operating in the New Territories; and blue, for the ones that operate only on Lantau Island. The drivers are efficient, although not necessarily friendly, and they sometimes speak only broken English. However, they know the city like the back of their hand, and they often take corners at high speed. I've come across a few extraordinary drivers, especially in Sai Kung. One day, my brother and I were waiting for a bus that would never come, because it only ran on Saturdays (and it wasn't Saturday). But Salomon, a taxicab driver, had been watching us wait for nothing and offered to take us although he was no longer on duty. On the way, he told us a lot of stories about Sai Kung.

NOVA
LIGHT BUS 19 SEATS
八合里

# LANTAU PEAK

## *ADA*

My choices for travel or hiking destinations can at times be a little superficial and might be based on a gorgeous Windows wallpaper, for example, or three stunning photographs I saw on a travel blog. Although I know full well that a few photos don't tell the whole story of a destination, I sometimes get taken in.

It was after reading a blog post that I decided to climb Lantau Peak. Having woken up early one day—by chance—I decided on a whim to climb Hong Kong's second-highest mountain, which is on Lantau Island.

The first several feet were pleasantly sheltered from the sun by trees, making it a cool start to the climb. The steps were uneven, unlike the "clean" ones you find on The Twins hike (see page 101), although I actually prefer the wilder conditions. I never wear headphones when I hike, and my climb that day was accompanied by the chirping of happy birds.

The path slowly opened up, offering a glimpse of what lay ahead: one upward stretch, followed by a second, and then a third . . . As I climbed, the magnificent landscape of Hong Kong's outlying islands gradually unfolded on my left. Between the turquoise of the sea and sky, the islands always give me the impression of turtle shells peeking out of the water. I was able to make out the islands of Cheung Chau, Shek Kwu Chau, Tai A Chau, and Siu A Chau. Behind me rose Sunset Peak, Lantau's next-highest mountain, which, as you might imagine, is magnificent at sunset.

As I contemplated that dual landscape, I couldn't help but think that Lantau Peak was Hong Kong in a nutshell: urban development pushed to the limit, alongside the mountains, the islands, peace and quiet, and the birds.

To my left, the water below me was still turquoise, and I could still see the white sand and the sea, with its crystal clear edges. To the right, between the mist and the mountains, I began to make out the apartment buildings that are so typical of Hong Kong. Next, the airport appeared, reminding me that I was still on Lantau Island.

As I contemplated that dual landscape, I couldn't help but think that Lantau Peak was Hong Kong in a nutshell: urban development pushed to the limit (I could see construction work going on, and the buildings were probably about to grow like mushrooms again), alongside the mountains, the islands, peace and quiet, and the birds.

After descending, I came to the park where the Big Buddha is located. Ahead was a huge Buddha statue perched at the top of the mountain. At its foot were crowds and a souvenir shop every several feet.

I quickly passed through that scene, which was too crowded for my liking; this return to reality was brutal. I decided to take the cable car back down the mountain to Tung Chung. From my glass cabin, I could take one last look at the summit of Lantau, the sea, and the scenery before descending deep into the bowels of the MTR station for the ride back to Central.

2 PM / 5 PM →

AFTERNOON SNACK

# 點心

# 咖喱魚蛋

# CURRY FISH BALLS

**Serves 3 to 4**
**Preparation time 10 minutes**
**Cooking time 15 minutes**

- 5¼ ounces (150 g) fish balls (available at Asian grocery stores)
- 1 tablespoon curry paste
- 1 tablespoon satay sauce
- 1 teaspoon chu hou paste
- ½ teaspoon ground turmeric
- 2 teaspoons garlic
- 1 tablespoon shallot
- 1 tablespoon oyster sauce
- ½ teaspoon sugar
- ¼ teaspoon salt
- ½ teaspoon chicken bouillon (stock) powder
- 1 tablespoon light soy sauce
- 1 tablespoon Shaoxing wine
- 1 teaspoon cornstarch (cornflour)
- Vegetable oil
- Salt and pepper

**This is traditional Hong Kong street food. These little fish paste balls are cooked to a slightly chewy consistency, then topped with a rich, fragrant curry sauce, made from a blend of spices and curry powder. Each stall has its own unique flavor combination. *(Davina)***

Bring a large pot of water to a boil. Add the fish balls, bring back to a boil, and drain.

Mix together the curry paste, satay sauce, chu hou paste, and turmeric until smooth.

Chop the garlic and shallot. Heat a wok with 2 tablespoons of oil and sauté the chopped garlic and shallot to release their aroma. Add the sauce and turmeric mixture and combine. Stir in ⅔ cup (150 ml) of hot water. Add the fish balls and the oyster sauce, sugar, salt, chicken bouillon powder, soy sauce, and Shaoxing wine. Stir, then bring to a boil over high heat. Reduce the heat to medium-low and simmer for 5 to 8 minutes.

Taste and adjust the seasoning with salt and pepper, if necessary. Add the cornstarch to thicken the sauce and serve immediately.

# CHEUNG FUN

## RICE NOODLE ROLLS WITH TWO SAUCES

**Serves 2 hungry schoolchildren (or 4 adults)**

**Preparation time 10 minutes**
**Cooking time 10 minutes**

- 1 tablespoon unhulled sesame seeds
- 1 package plain rice noodle rolls (available at Asian grocery stores)
- 1 scallion (spring onion)
- 2 tablespoons peanut butter
- ½ teaspoon sugar
- 2 tablespoons light soy sauce
- 1 teaspoon hoisin sauce

**One day, I saw a group of schoolchildren lined up at a tiny food stall near the Wan Chai MTR station. They were all excited as they gave their orders, which the cook prepared and handed to them in less than 2 minutes, and together they all relished their steaming rice noodle rolls. It occurred to me for a moment that I would rather have been a schoolgirl in Hong Kong having *cheung fun* as an afternoon snack than one in Paris having Kiri® cheese sandwiches. *(Ada)***

Toast the sesame seeds in a dry skillet (frying pan) over medium heat.

Steam the rice noodle rolls according to the package directions.

Chop the scallion.

In a bowl over a bain-marie (hot water bath) or double boiler, mix the peanut butter and sugar with 1 tablespoon water.

In a separate bowl, mix together the soy sauce and hoisin sauce with 1 tablespoon of water.

Drain any moisture from the cooked rice noodle rolls and serve with the two sauces, toasted sesame seeds, and chopped scallion.

# DAN TAAT



## EGG TARTS

**Makes 12**
**Preparation time 15 minutes**
**Resting time 30 minutes**
**Cooking time 30 minutes**

- 1¾ cups plus 1½ tablespoons (230 g) cake (Italian '00') flour
- ⅔ cup (145 g) butter
- ½ cup (60 g) confectioners' (icing) sugar
- ¼ teaspoon salt
- 3 eggs
- ⅓ cup (70 g) granulated sugar
- 1½ tablespoons (25 g) evaporated milk
- ½ teaspoon vanilla extract

**When I arrived in Paris, I was captivated by *flan pâtissier*, basically a French custard tart. Although simple, it was so delicious that I took one with me on a 12-hour flight back to Hong Kong, just so my mother could taste one. "It's almost like a big egg tart," she concluded. I suddenly realized why I loved it so much: it reminded me of my favorite afternoon snack, egg tarts. *(Davina)***

To make the dough, mix the flour with the cubed butter, confectioners' sugar, and salt. Gently rub the butter into the dry ingredients with your hands to form coarse crumbs. Add 1 egg and gently work with the palm of your hand to form a smooth dough. Cover with plastic wrap (cling film) and refrigerate for 30 minutes to allow the flour to absorb the moisture.

Make a syrup by dissolving the sugar in ⅔ cup (165 ml) of hot water, then let cool.

Beat 2 eggs with the evaporated milk and vanilla until smooth. Add the syrup and continue to beat. Strain the mixture two times through a fine-mesh strainer (sieve) into a liquid measuring cup (jug) for pouring. The mixture should be perfectly smooth.

Preheat the oven to 375°F (190°C/Gas Mark 5).

On a lightly floured work surface, roll out the pastry to a thickness of about ⅛ inch (4 mm). Lay a sheet of parchment (baking) paper on top and run a rolling pin over to be sure of an even thickness. Using a 3¼-inch (8-cm)-diameter cookie cutter, cut out 12 disks.

Carefully place a pastry disk in the center of a mini tart pan (with a diameter of 2 inches/5 cm at the bottom and 2¾ inches/7 cm at the top, ¾ inch/2 cm deep). Line the pan by pressing the pastry with your fingers against the bottom and sides, stretching as little as possible. Leave a margin of about 1/16 inch (2 mm) above the rim to allow for shrinkage when baked. Repeat the process with all the disks and place the molds on a baking sheet.

Carefully pour the custard filling into each tart shell (case) and bake for 25 to 27 minutes, until a toothpick (cocktail stick) inserted into the center comes out clean. Let the tarts cool for 5 to 10 minutes before unmolding (they should release easily). Serve while still warm, accompanied by a nice milk tea (see page 32).

# THE EGG TART, A HONG KONG ICON
## *ADA*

Anyone who has ever set foot in Hong Kong will tell you that the city is full of bakeries, and that their windows are filled with egg tarts: round tarts with a canary yellow filling. Some 13,000 egg tarts are made each day in Hong Kong, so they are difficult to ignore.

The first time I ever tasted a Hong Kong-style egg tart was actually in Paris, at Bing Sutt. Despite several visits to Hong Kong, I'd never really been drawn to this pastry. And yet, my first bite into the crispy pastry and warm and comforting filling was an almost overwhelming experience. In fact, I stopped talking to the person sitting across from me so that I could finish enjoying the little gem.

While there is no real historical record to speak of regarding this pastry, the egg tart is thought to have various origins during the colonial period.

Some attribute its appearance to Guangzhou in the 1940s. At the time, it was the only port to welcome travelers from all over the world, including English travelers. A Cantonese chef is said to have appropriated the English custard tart and adapted it to use the ingredients available: lard or pork fat instead of butter, and a mixture of eggs and milk imitating custard, but less liquid. It is also said that one restaurant replaced shortcrust pastry with the puff pastry that was being used for another recipe.

Some 13,000 egg tarts are made each day in Hong Kong, so they are difficult to ignore.

Another version is that egg tart was derived from the custard tarts that are made in neighboring Macau (which has the same special administrative region status as Hong Kong). The custard tart made in Macau, which has a more caramelized top, dates from the period when it was a colony of Portugal (until 1999). This mini tart is reminiscent of the world-famous Portuguese *pastel de nata*. In this case, it would have traveled from Portugal to Macau before reaching Hong Kong.

Like most restaurant dishes in the 1940s and up to the 1950s, the egg tart was reserved for the more affluent social classes and foreigners.

However, in about 1960, with the decline in British power and loss of Hong Kongers' purchasing power, the egg tart became accessible to the masses and found its way onto the menus of the city's restaurants and into bakeries. This was in response to the need for food that would be easy, fast, and inexpensive to both produce and eat, and this is why it is still so popular today.

# 奶茶蛋撻

# MILK TEA EGG TARTS

**Makes 10**
**Preparation time 35 minutes**
**Resting time 1 hour**
**Cooking time 2 hours 55 minutes**

1 (14-ounce/400-g) can plus 1½ tablespoons (25 g) condensed milk

¾ cup plus 2 tablespoons (200 g) unsalted butter

⅓ cup plus 2 tablespoons (55 g) confectioners' (icing) sugar

⅓ cup (25 g) whole (full-fat) instant dry (powdered) milk

2⅓ cups plus 1 tablespoon (300 g) all-purpose (plain) flour

5 eggs

½ cup (100 g) granulated sugar

2 cups (500 ml) milk

⅓ cup (25 g) Ceylon tea

**Tuesday, 10 a.m. I'm at Tai On, sitting in one of the booths and drinking an iced *yuen yeung*. Thursday, 11:33 a.m. I'm eating scallion noodles with a crispy fried egg at Tai On, leafing through a battered old book on waffles. Saturday, 3:17 p.m. I'm at the counter of Tai On waiting for my favorite milk tea egg tart, of which I've eaten many. At 4:04 p.m., I leave Tai On with a package of postcards featuring some of Hong Kong's neighborhoods and their specialties, and I take a last look at the shop window where taro egg tarts, matcha egg tarts, taro and Ovaltine, and peanut butter egg tarts are proudly lined up on their trays, illuminated by the sun as though under a spotlight. Many thanks to Tiffany and the pastry chef, who agreed to share the recipe. *(Ada)***

Place the can of condensed milk in a saucepan filled with water and simmer over low heat for 2 hours 30 minutes. Let cool, open the can, and transfer the caramel to a pastry (piping) bag.

Cut the butter into cubes and beat them with the confectioners' sugar. Stir in the 1½ tablespoons (25 g) of condensed milk, then incorporate the instant milk and flour.

Divide the pastry into ten 2-ounce (55-g) pieces and line 10 mini tart pans (3 inches/7.5 cm in diameter and 1½ inches/4 cm deep), pressing so it is even. Pipe caramel to cover the bottom of the tart shells (cases) and refrigerate for 30 minutes.

Preheat the oven to 350°F (180°C/Gas Mark 4).

Beat the eggs, then add the granulated sugar and combine. Heat the milk with the tea until just steaming, then turn off the heat. Let cool. Strain and incorporate the milk tea into the beaten eggs. Strain again to remove any air bubbles, then fill the tart shells with the mixture.

Place the mini tarts on a baking sheet lined with parchment (baking) paper. Bake for about 25 minutes, or until the tip of a knife comes out dry. Let cool for 20 minutes, unmold, and serve.

# 芒果糯米糍

2 P.M. / 5 P.M.

# MANGO MOCHI

**Makes 4**
**Preparation time 20 minutes**
**Refrigeration time 20 minutes**
**Cooking time 25 minutes**

1 cup (160 g) glutinous rice flour (ground sticky rice)

⅓ cup (80 ml) milk

⅔ cup (160 ml) coconut milk

¼ cup (45 g) sugar

2½ tablespoons (20 g) cornstarch (cornflour)

1 tablespoon vegetable oil

2 ripe mangoes

**My brother, who had previously recommended I go to Cheung Chau, also urged me to try the island's specialty, mango mochi (see page 12). Instead of being small and round with a thin skin, the mochi made in Cheung Chau is plump and fits well in the palm of your hand, kind of like Beyoncé at the Superbowl. Its skin is thick, and the fruit is cut into large chunks, enabling you to completely enjoy its juice, tartness, and consistent, tender flesh. To reproduce the delicious flavor of Cheung Chau mango mochi, use particularly ripe mangoes—it's better if they are overripe rather than underripe. *(Ada)***

Toast ¼ cup (40 g) of the rice flour in a dry skillet (frying pan) over medium heat for a few minutes.

Mix the milk, coconut milk, and sugar, then add the remaining rice flour and cornstarch and mix vigorously. Press the dough through a strainer (sieve) to remove any lumps.

Cover the dough with plastic wrap (clingfilm) and steam for 25 minutes. To check that the dough is cooked enough, prick it with a chopstick; it should come out dry.

Add the oil and work the dough vigorously with a fork. It should become supple, elastic, and glossy.

Cover with plastic wrap and refrigerate for about 20 minutes. This will make the dough easier to use.

Remove the mango cheeks. Scoop out the flesh in one piece with a spoon.

Divide the dough into 4 pieces. Because the dough is sticky, you should wear gloves when handling it. Place 1 piece of dough between 2 sheets of plastic wrap and roll out flat. Place the flesh of one mango cheek in the center, then wrap and seal. Roll the mochi in the toasted rice flour. Repeat the process to make the other three mochi.

If you aren't planning to eat the mochi immediately, they should be placed in paper muffin liners (cases) to keep them from sticking to each other or to the storage container.

Mochi will keep for 2 days in the refrigerator.

## NOTE

Toasting the glutinous rice flour reduces its floury texture, which can be unpleasant when eaten. It also makes it easier to digest, so don't skip this step!

# CHEUNG CHAU
## *ADA*

I'm usually the one who gives my brother advice, because despite how much I love him, he doesn't always have the best ideas. However, after spending a week in Hong Kong (without me), he said to me, "Ada, the next time you come, you absolutely must go to Cheung Chau. You'll love it." I took his word for it. So, one sunny Thursday in April, I disembarked from the ferry at 11 o'clock in the morning.

The island is the site of a festival that is well known to all Hong Kongers, the Tai Ping Jiao Festival, or Cheng Chau Bun Festival.

Before even thinking about visiting anything, I heeded my little brother's second piece of advice: try a mango mochi, the island's specialty. Unlike the filled mochi cake made in Japan, which is smaller and rounder, the one made on Cheung Chau is long—you practically need two hands to hold it—and filled with a large piece of fruit.

I headed for the Po Tsai Cave, named after the pirate Cheung Po Tsai, who operated under the Qing dynasty (mainly between 1800 and 1810) and is said to have hidden his treasures there. Provided you aren't claustrophobic or afraid of the dark (which, luckily, I'm not), you can venture into the cave, more than 30 feet (10 m) underground, and emerge on the other side just a few minutes later.

I headed back down the coastal path, past the Lutheran village, and came across three old ladies on a bench who burst out laughing when they saw me. They said a lot of things to me in Cantonese that I didn't understand, so I pointed to the little street I was thinking of taking, as if to ask if I should continue in that direction. "Yes, yes," they answered with such gusto that I took it (in fact, it was the way to the public restroom).

It was time for an afternoon snack. At the end of the island, not far from a bookstore where I found a few rare books in English, I sat down at a *bing sutt* and ordered a sweet mango soup with coconut, red beans, and glutinous rice pearls. The manager brought me my food and then sat down next to me, all smiles, and asked me what brought me to Cheung Chau. I replied that I had come to explore the island because it was my first time there. In perfect English, he continued: "So, seeing that you've been here all day, you probably noticed the buns everywhere. Do you know what they are?" Actually, I had taken note of those perfectly round, white or sometimes pink buns, stamped with a red Chinese character.

He explained that the red character means "peace." This particular bun is the emblem of Cheung Chau. The island is the site of a festival that is well known to all Hong Kongers, the Tai Ping Jiao Festival, or Cheng Chau Bun Festival, which dates back to the eighteenth century. It was originally celebrated by the island's fishermen to pray for protection against pirates. It has since become a tourist attraction and lost all religious connotations.

The festivities include several events, such as a parade of floats and a bun-scrambling competition, which involves scrambling up one of the 40-feet (13-m)-tall towers that are covered by as many as 18,000 buns, to snatch as many buns as possible and, above all, to be the first to reach the top.

I was right to listen to my brother's advice. Now it's up to me to make him promise to come back, if possible, during the Bun Festival—and to have one for me.

Cheung Chau Beach Road
長洲東堤路

# TAI O
## *ADA*

One day, I saw a magnificent Swiss castle on my boyfriend's computer screen. A few weeks later, I was dragging him to Switzerland, where we took one train, then another, and then walked, until we arrived at Chillon Castle. I finally had the Windows wallpaper in front of me.

Another day, I saw a story on Instagram about a fishing village in Hong Kong that I had never been to or knew anything about. A few weeks later, I took two planes, then a bus, a subway, and a ferry, before boarding a final bus that ran along the south coast of Lantau Island to Tai O.

There I was, staring at the photograph from that Instagram story (posted by somebody I didn't even know). This village of canals and houses on stilts in the village had been a gateway to Hong Kong decades earlier for Chinese refugees escaping the mainland during the Chinese Civil War.

Tai O felt like being in another era; there were no buses, cars, or high-rises. The houses were perched on wooden stilts, each with its own boat attached to a pole, and there were sampans (a type of boat) painted canary yellow, strawberry red, azure blue, and apple green. Large orange awnings sheltered stalls selling dried fish, jars of shrimp paste, and XO sauce adorned with handwritten labels squeezed between fish bladders and bags of salted cuttlefish.

> Tai O felt like being in another era; the houses were perched on wooden stilts, each with its own boat attached to a pole, and there were sampans painted canary yellow, strawberry red, azure blue, and apple green.

There was a waft of curry, and I could see a man busy at his pot, preparing his fish balls. A little way along, on a jetty, I stopped for a while to contemplate egg yolks drying on braided mats under the sun. I thought they were beautiful; the salt had caused yellow dots to appear on the brilliant orange of the gleaming yolks. The salted and dried egg yolks are prized for their nourishing properties for the blood and spleen, and in Chinese medicine they are used to strengthen the vital energy known as *qi*.

The weather turned cloudy and I returned to the center of the village. At a stall, I bought the bag of dried shrimp my brother had asked for. I considered picking up a jar of XO sauce (page 186), because I had heard that the best was to be found at Tai O. But my suitcase was already so full that I decided against it.

Then I gulped down a doughnut while enjoying my last few minutes there, before boarding a bus, a subway train, another subway train, and a minibus for the journey back.

每個
4元
justjoy
佳記

# TAI O DOUGHNUTS

**Makes 6 (just enough for me)**
**Preparation time 10 minutes**
**Resting time 30 minutes**
**Cooking time 45 minutes**

5¾ tablespoons (80 g) butter
¼ cup (50 g) plus 1 teaspoon sugar
¾ cup plus 1 tablespoon (100 g) all-purpose (plain) flour
3 eggs
Oil for deep-frying

**I tried my first Tai O doughnut, or sugar egg puff, while sitting on the ground on a rainy and truly gloomy day in Tai O. I had just bought it from a lady who couldn't have been much older than my mother. She had a most uncluttered stall, consisting of a stainless steel worktop and a deep fryer, right in the middle of an alley. I instantly wanted to take shelter inside the soft and warm air pockets of this doughnut.** ***(Ada)***

In a saucepan, melt the butter and dissolve 1 teaspoon of the sugar in ⅓ cup plus 1½ tablespoons (100 ml) of water. Remove it from the heat and add the flour all at once. Mix well to a smooth paste.

Beat the eggs and add gradually, stirring continuously, to incorporate. The resulting dough should be smooth, glossy, and a little sticky. Cover with a cloth and let rest for 30 minutes.

It is best to cook the doughnuts in a deep fryer, because you can control the temperature. The oil temperature should not exceed 285°F (140°C), otherwise the doughnuts will become too hard and dark.

Using 2 large spoons, shape pieces of dough into balls and add to the simmering oil (no more than three at a time, because the doughnuts will puff up considerably when cooked). Cook the doughnuts for 20 minutes, keeping an eye on them and turning them, if necessary.

Roll the cooked doughnuts in sugar and serve immediately. They should be eaten right away, even if hot.

# QQ芝士波波
# QQ CHEESE BALLS

**Makes 16**
**Preparation time 30 minutes**
**Cooking time 35 minutes**

¼ cup (30 g) bread (strong) flour
1½ tablespoons (20 g) sugar
½ teaspoon salt
⅔ cup (160 ml) milk
2 tablespoons (30 g) butter
⅔ cup (90 g) tapioca starch
3 tablespoons (30 g) glutinous rice flour (ground sticky rice)
1 extra-large (UK large) egg
⅓ cup (30 g) grated fresh Parmesan cheese
¼ cup (30 g) shredded cheddar cheese

**In recent years, QQ balls have become a staple of almost every bakery in Hong Kong. They were first introduced as a savory and cheesy snack, but, over time, bakers have experimented with new flavors and introduced sweet versions, including chocolate, matcha, and Earl Grey tea flavors. The options are now endless. But what exactly does "QQ" mean? QQ is a Taiwanese acronym for a soft and springy texture, which is what makes these little treats irresistible. They make the perfect snack for any occasion. I remember hiking up Lion Rock with my best friend. By the time we reached the top, we were both exhausted and delighted. As I caught my breath, she smiled and pulled a large bag of QQ balls from her backpack. "This is the best reward after this climb." She was absolutely right. *(Davina)***

In a bowl, make a batter by mixing the bread flour, sugar, and salt together, then gradually incorporate the milk.

Melt the butter in a nonstick skillet (frying pan) over medium heat. Add the batter to the skillet, stirring continuously to prevent lumps from forming. Continue to cook until the mixture thickens, then remove from the heat.

Add the cornstarch and rice flour and mix with a spatula until smooth.

Beat the egg and gradually incorporate into the dough (in at least 5 or 6 additions), mixing well after each addition, until the dough forms a stiff peak when the spatula is lifted. You may not need to use the whole egg.

Add the cheeses and stir until fully incorporated. Transfer the dough to a pastry bag and cut a 2-cm-wide hole.

Preheat the oven to 350°F (180°C/Gas Mark 4). Line a baking sheet with parchment (baking) paper.

Pipe balls of dough with a diameter of about 1½ inches (4 cm) onto the baking sheet, then bake for about 30 minutes. If the balls shrink when taken out of the oven, it means that they are not completely cooked on the inside. In this case, return them to the oven for 5 to 10 minutes.

QQ cheese balls are best served hot.

# 紙杯蛋糕

# PAPER-WRAPPED SPONGE CAKES

**Makes 4 to 6**
**Preparation time 20 minutes**
**Cooking time 25 minutes**

3 eggs
⅓ cup (60 g) sugar
2½ tablespoons (40 ml) vegetable oil
¼ cup (70 ml) whole (full-fat) milk
⅔ cup (80 g) cake (Italian '00') flour
1½ tablespoons (10 g) cornstarch (cornflour)
1¾ teaspoons (10 g) custard powder (optional)

**Like pineapple buns and egg tarts, paper-wrapped sponge cakes originated in the 1950s, while Hong Kong was under British colonial rule, at a time when most inhabitants had modest incomes but were drawn to Western-style desserts. To meet this demand, local replaced expensive ingredients with local alternatives— for example, butter with oil. However, more than the simplicity of its ingredients, what is amazing is the incredibly light texture and intense egg flavor of this cake, a childhood delight cherished by all Hong Kongers! *(Davina)***

Preheat the oven to 340°F (170°C/Gas Mark 3½). Line the cups of a muffin pan with muffin liners (cases). For a more authentic look, you can use parchment (baking) paper squares.

Separate the whites from the yolks.

Whisk the yolks with 1½ tablespoons (20 g) of the sugar. Add the oil and milk, then whisk until smooth. Add the flour, cornstarch, and custard powder, then mix to a smooth batter.

Using a handheld mixer, beat the egg whites until foamy. Add the remaining sugar in three additions while beating the whites to soft peaks. Fold the beaten egg whites into the dough, one-third at a time.

Fill the liners to three-quarters with the batter and bake for 20 to 25 minutes. Let cool on a rack.

# 炸雞髀

# FRIED CHICKEN LEGS

**Serves 2**
**Preparation time 10 minutes**
**Marinating time 4 hours**
**Cooking time 25 minutes**

2 large chicken legs
4¼ cups (1 liter) oil for deep-frying
Salt and pepper

**FOR THE MARINADE:**

⅓ cup plus 1 tablespoon (50 g) all-purpose (plain) flour
⅓ cup plus 1 tablespoon (50 g) cornstarch (cornflour)
3 tablespoons (40 g) plain (natural) yogurt
1 tablespoon light soy sauce
1 tablespoon Worcestershire sauce
1 tablespoon vegetable oil
1 tablespoon Shaoxing wine
2 teaspoons Chinese five-spice powder
1 teaspoon salt
1 teaspoon white pepper
1 teaspoon sugar
1 extra-large (UK large) egg

Mix all the marinade ingredients in a bowl. Cover the chicken legs in the marinade and refrigerate for at least 4 hours (ideally overnight).

On the actual day, bring the chicken legs to room temperature.

Heat the frying oil in a large saucepan over medium heat to 325°F (160°C).

Carefully place one chicken leg in the oil, skin side down, and fry for 5 minutes. Remove from the oil and let cool for 2 minutes, then return to the oil, skin side up this time. Fry for another 5 minutes, until both sides are golden and crisp. Drain on a rack and repeat with the other leg. Season and serve immediately.

# MONG KOK AND THE HONG KONG STREET FOOD CULTURE

## *DAVINA*

If I had to pick the neighborhood I spent the most time hanging out with my friends in during high school, it would definitely be Mong Kok. This bustling district is home to some of Hong Kong's best street food and is the perfect place for a snack after school. Which ones do I consider indispensable? Curried fish balls and egg waffles, the latter being simple but truly satisfying. Mong Kok was where I first discovered bagged noodles (see page 154), a true Hong Kong experience. These are egg noodles that are drizzled with a soy and garlic sauce and served ready to eat in a small plastic bag. You eat them as you walk using bamboo skewers as improvised chopsticks—a real test of dexterity. At the time, they barely cost 10 Hong Kong dollars, so they made the perfect snack to get me through to dinner. The experience was also enough to keep me coming back to Mong Kok again and again.

Mong Kok is also where I learned to appreciate the street food that foreigners might find surprising. The mention of street food usually brings to mind the typical fish balls or *siu mai* (see page 84), but it goes far beyond these traditional dishes. Aside from them, there are also organ meat (offal) skewers made from pork intestines, beef tripe, or chicken gizzards, among many others. While this type of street food may seem challenging to some, for me, it's just another facet of the city's culinary landscape. It's an acquired taste, but once you have it, it is something you'll crave. Some evenings, my mother and I would buy a dozen skewers, and that would be enough for dinner.

Mong Kok is a true reflection of Hong Kong and its mix of chaos, energy, and unique charm. Each street has its own atmosphere, where the smells of street food is mingled with the neon signs of electronics stores and market stalls. It's a neighborhood that never sleeps. Perhaps this is the reason it was used as the setting for some of the most memorable scenes in Wong Kar-Wai's cult movie *In the Mood for Love.*

This bustling district is home to some of Hong Kong's best street food.

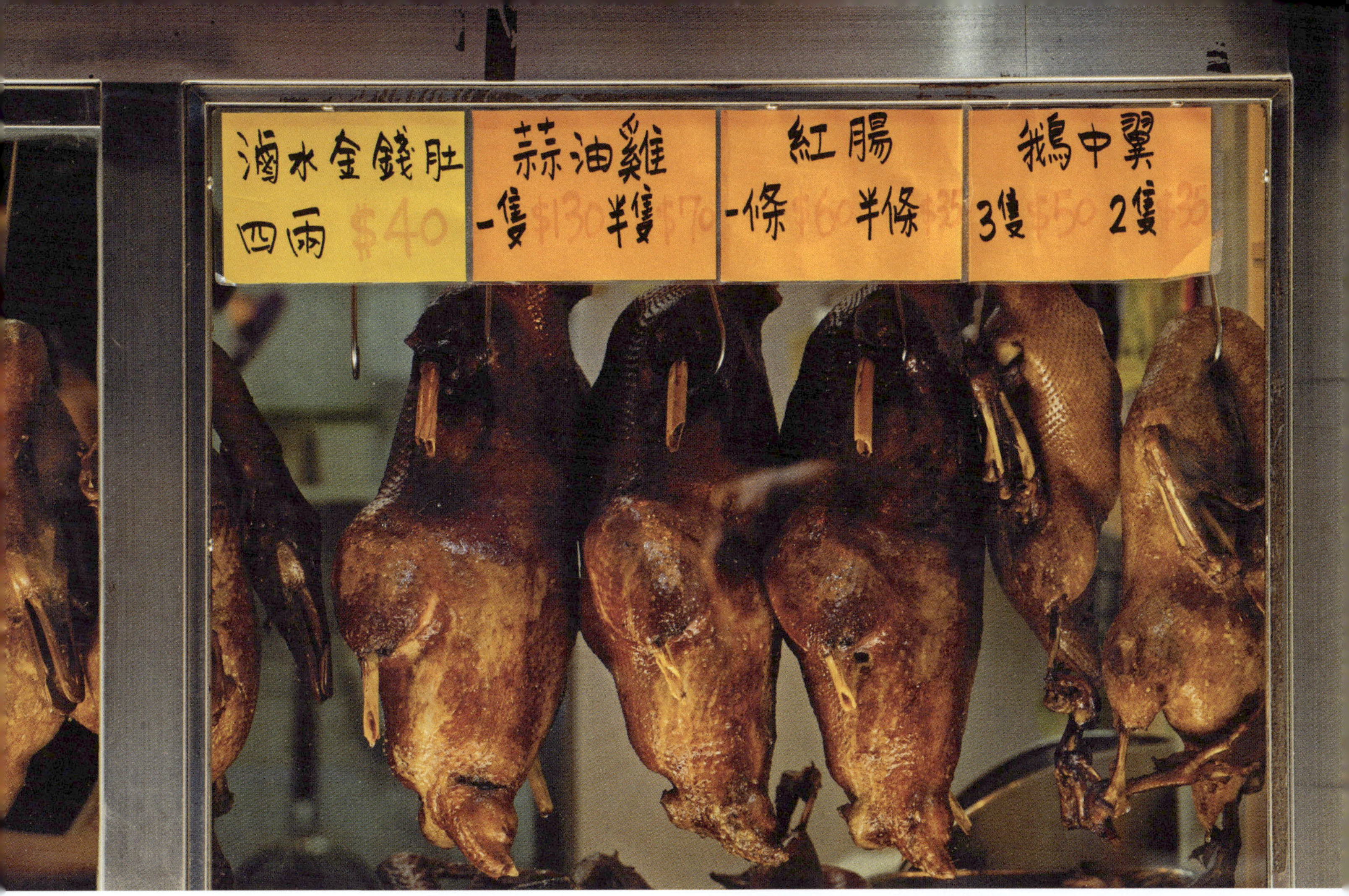
滷水金錢肚
四兩 $40
蒜油雞
一隻 $130 半隻 $70
紅腸
一條 $60 半條
鵝中翼
3隻 $50 2隻

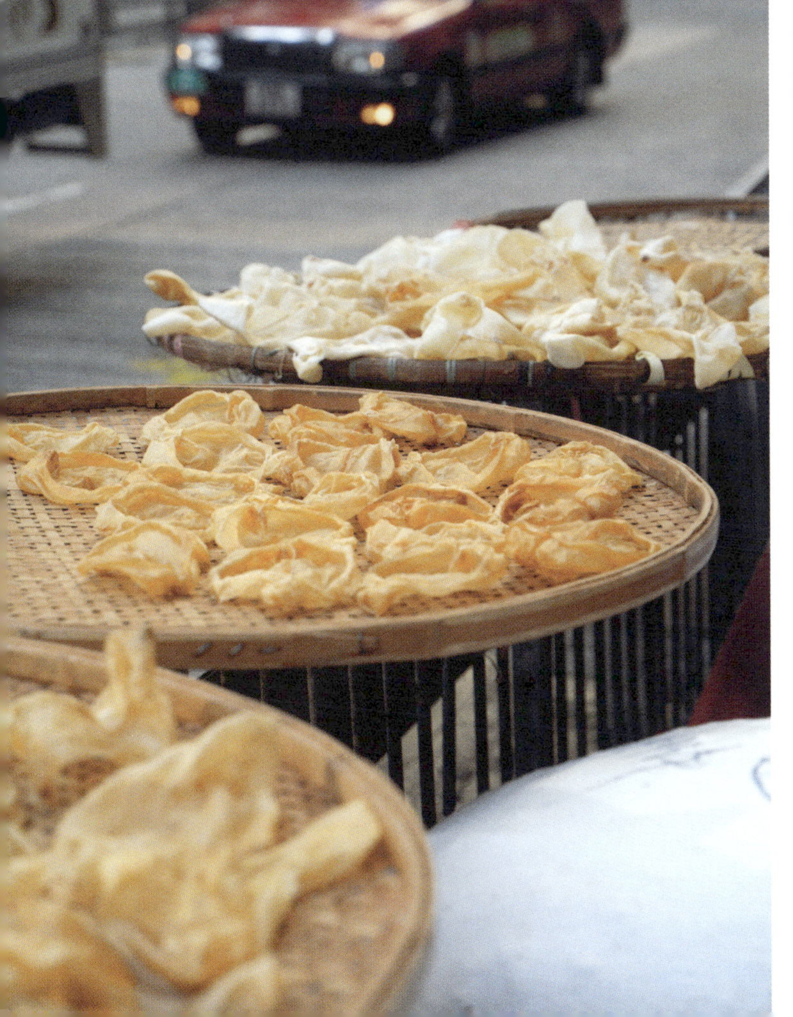

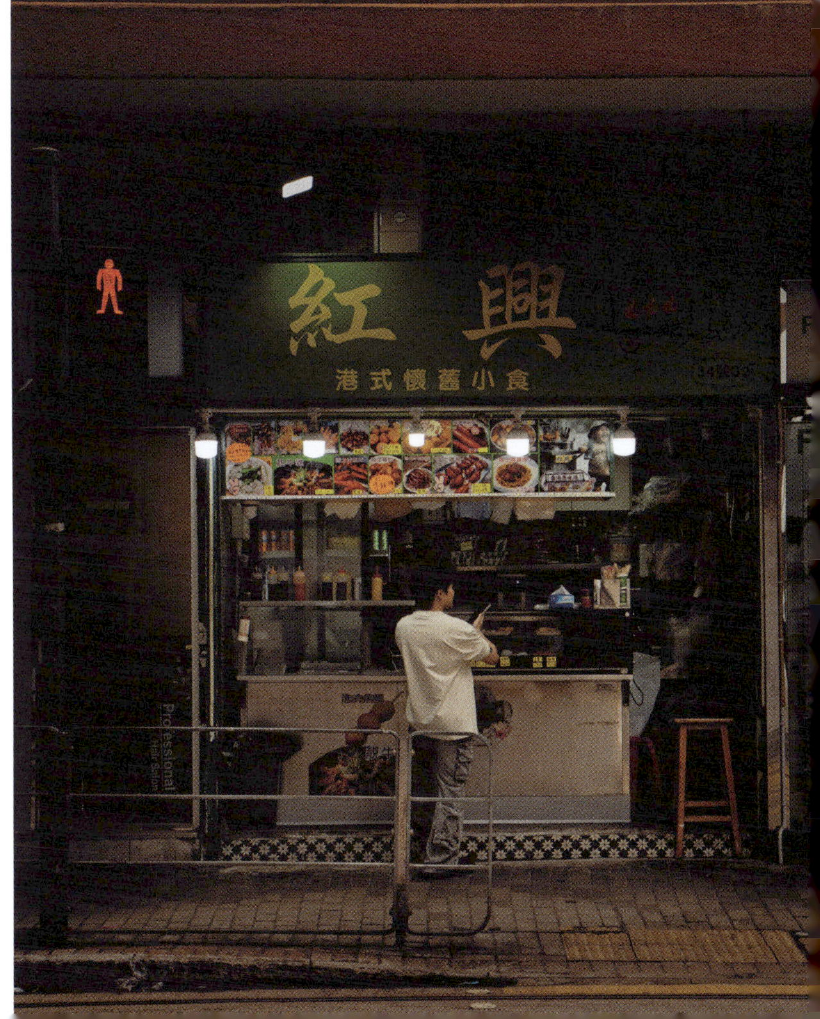

紅興
港式懷舊小食

# GAI DAN ZAI

## EGG WAFFLES ("EGGETTES")

**Serves 4**
**Preparation time 15 minutes**
**Resting time 1 hour**
**Cooking time 4 minutes per waffle**

1 cup (125 g) all-purpose (plain) flour
1 teaspoon baking powder
2 tablespoons tapioca starch
1 tablespoon custard powder
2 eggs
⅔ cup (130 g) sugar
2 tablespoons evaporated milk
1 tablespoon vegetable oil
1 teaspoon vanilla extract
Choice of flavorings: Sesame seeds, chocolate chips, matcha powder, etc. (optional)

**If you were to ask me for my favorite snack in Hong Kong, it would definitely be egg waffles. Every time I step out of the Wan Chai MTR station, I find myself irresistibly drawn to the delicious aroma of eggs wafting through the air, leading me straight to a nearby street food vendor. Before you know it, I'm holding a hot waffle in my hand. Eggettes, as these waffles are also popularly known, have spread around the world in recent years. They are often served with ice cream or whipped cream. In Hong Kong, however, nothing beats the original waffles, with their rich egg flavor and unique texture of being crispy on the outside and soft on the inside.** ***(Davina)***

In a bowl, mix together the flour, baking powder, cornstarch, and custard.

Beat the eggs with the sugar, then gradually incorporate the evaporated milk and ⅔ cup (150 ml) of water. Mix well. Stir in the flour mixture to form a smooth batter. Add the oil and vanilla and mix to combine. At this stage, you can add any flavorings, if desired.

Cover the bowl with plastic wrap (clingfilm) and refrigerate for at least 1 hour.

Place a waffle iron over medium heat and grease the plates with oil.

Add the batter, close, and flip. Cook for 2 minutes, then flip again and cook for another 2 minutes. Carefully remove the waffle and place it on a rack. Repeat the process to use all the remaining batter, oiling the plates each time.

These waffles are best served freshly made. They will become crisp as they cool down.

2 P.M. / 5 P.M.

# BOOT JAI GO

## RED BEAN PUDDINGS

**Makes 4**
**Preparation time 25 minutes**
**Soaking time 6 to 8 hours**
**Cooking time 1 hour 5 minutes**

⅓ cup (60 g) red (adzuki) beans
½ cup (70 g) rice flour (ground rice)
2½ tablespoons (20 g) wheat starch
2 tablespoons (15 g) cornstarch (cornflour)
¼ cup (60 g) packed (soft) brown sugar

**Steamed red bean pudding is a type of street food that dates from the 1940s. They were traditionally made in earthenware bowls, hence the name *(boot* [缽]means "bowl" and *go* [糕] means "cake"). When I was a kid, I would wait impatiently for the vendor to remove the pudding from its bowl using a pair of bamboo skewers before giving it to me. *(Davina)***

Soak the beans for 6 to 8 hours, preferably overnight. On the actual day, drain and cook the beans in boiling water for about 45 minutes, then drain again (you can also buy cooked and canned beans at most Asian grocery stores).

In a bowl, mix the rice flour, wheat starch, and cornstarch. Add scant 1 cup (200 ml) of water and mix well.

Make a syrup by gently heating ⅓ cup plus 1½ tablespoons (100 ml) of water in a saucepan, then add the sugar and stir until completely dissolved.

Add the syrup to the batter and mix until smooth.

Oil four small bowls (⅔-cup/150-ml capacity each) and heat in a steamer for 5 minutes. This will make it easier to unmold the puddings.

Put about 1 ½ teaspoons cooked red beans into each bowl, then fill with the batter. Place the bowls back in the steamer and cook for 20 minutes, until an inserted toothpick (cocktail stick) comes out clean.

Let cool and serve with bamboo skewers for the full Hong Kong experience.

2 P.M. / 5 P.M.

# RED BEAN ICE

**Serves 2**
**Preparation time 20 minutes**
**Soaking time overnight**
**Cooking time 1 hour 30 minutes**
**Refrigeration time 2 hours**

¾ cup (150 g) red (adzuki) beans

5½ ounces (160 g) Chinese rock sugar (available in Chinese grocery stores) or sugar lumps (or ¾ cup/160 g granulated sugar)

½ cup (120 ml) evaporated milk (or coconut milk)

20 ice cubes

2 scoops vanilla ice cream (optional)

**This dessert and beverage in one offers a complete sensory experience as you stir the ice, scoop up red beans from the bottom, and watch the stunning red and white colors slowly merge. This refreshment, which originated in the 1960s to combat Hong Kong's sweltering, humid heat, is still served in the city's *cha chaan tengs* and continues to delight both young and old. *(Davina)***

Soak the beans in plenty of water overnight.

On the actual day, rinse and drain the beans. Add to a saucepan with 4¼ cups (1 liter) of water, place over medium-high heat, and bring to a boil. Reduce the heat to medium-low and cook for 50 minutes, stirring occasionally.

Add the sugar and continue to cook for 30 to 40 minutes, until the beans are tender. Stir regularly during the final 10 minutes for even cooking. The mixture should form a thick paste, with half the beans left intact and the rest broken up. Remove from the heat, cover, and let cool to room temperature. Transfer the paste to an airtight container and refrigerate for at least 2 hours.

Fill 2 glasses halfway with bean paste and add the evaporated milk, filling the glasses to three-quarters full.

Crush the ice cubes in a blender and fill the glasses to the top with crushed ice. Add more evaporated milk, if necessary.

If desired, serve each glass topped with a scoop of vanilla ice cream.

# FOOD AS MEDICINE

## *DAVINA*

When I began to plan this book, I had a clear list of subjects I was eager to explore and share with readers interested in Hong Kong's culture and neighborhoods. However, one day as I was talking with a friend, and she encouraged me to include something I hadn't thought of: the use of food as medicine.

I can't count the number of times as a child I was told to finish my soup, because it would give me better skin; or to eat more goji berries to nourish my liver. I didn't care at the time, but as I grew older and felt the effects of the environment on my body, I gradually turned to the teachings that I hadn't realized were part of my daily life since childhood.

What I find amusing is that I can tell you what to eat at any time to cure any little problem. Are you feeling a little weak? Boil dates with goji berries. Is your internal heat too high,[14] or is your throat sore? Drink chrysanthemum tea. Do you have digestive issues? Steep (infuse) some fresh ginger in hot water. My boyfriend is still fascinated by all of this, but it has become second nature for me.

14. This is known in Chinese medicine as an imbalance in the Fire element.

Away from the family table, this view of food as medicine can also be found in Chinese herbal teas, which are a common sight on the streets of Hong Kong.

Away from the family table, this view of food as medicine can also be found in Chinese herbal teas, which are a common sight on the streets of Hong Kong. If you stroll through the city, you will often come across small, modest stores selling medicinal teas, with large bronze vessels lined up at the entrance and bowls of tea ready to be served. In Cantonese, these teas are called *leung cha* (涼茶), which means "refreshing tea." These ancestral concoctions are an integral part of Hong Kong's cultural heritage.

One thing that has always intrigued me is that medicinal tea stores also sell tea eggs (see page 150). Well known throughout Hong Kong, these are eggs simmered in a black tea flavored with star anise and other spices, giving them a deliciously rich and slightly woody taste. They are delicious!

$13
五花茶
祛濕清熱
明目養顏
消暑散熱

2 P.M. / 5 P.M.

# TEA EGGS

**Makes 12**
**Preparation time 15 minutes**
**Refrigeration time 24 hours**
**Cooking time 20 minutes**

12 eggs

**FOR THE MARINADE:**

¼ cup (60 ml) light soy sauce
2 tablespoons dark soy sauce
2 bay leaves
1 teaspoon Sichuan pepper
1 star anise
1 small cinnamon stick
2 teaspoons sugar
1 teaspoon salt
2 tablespoons black tea leaves

**Every afternoon at around four o'clock, students crowd around Hong Kong's street food stalls, eager to enjoy an afternoon snack. Undeniably, one of the most popular snacks is tea eggs, boiled eggs steeped (infused) in a fragrant tea-flavored marinade. *(Davina)***

The previous day, mix all marinade ingredients in a small saucepan with 2½ cups (600 ml) of water and bring to a boil over medium heat. Reduce the heat to low and let simmer for 10 minutes. Remove from the heat and let cool completely, then strain to remove the tea leaves.

Bring a large pot of water (enough to completely submerge the eggs) to a boil. Reduce the heat to low and, using a ladle, carefully lower the eggs into the water to prevent cracking. Cook for 10 minutes.

Immediately plunge the boiled eggs into a bowl of ice water for 2 to 3 minutes, or run cold water over them until they cool. By tapping gently with the back of a spoon, crack the shells all over without breaking through them completely.

Transfer the eggs to a freezer bag, fill with the marinade, and refrigerate for 24 hours.

On the actual day, peel the eggs just before serving. They can be served cold or at room temperature.

2 P.M. / 5 P.M.

# IMITATION SHARK FIN SOUP

**Serves 6**
**Preparation time 15 minutes**
**Soaking time 1 hour**
**Cooking time 15 to 20 minutes**

¼ cup (10 g) dried wood ear mushrooms

4 dried shiitake mushrooms

½ ounce (15 g) cellophane noodles (mung bean vermicelli)

1 tablespoon cornstarch (cornstarch)

6⅓ cups (1.5 liters) chicken (or pork) broth (stock)

1 tablespoon (5 g) fresh ginger

1⅓ cups (200 g) shredded, cooked chicken (or pork)

1 tablespoon Shaoxing wine

¼ teaspoon white pepper

½ teaspoon sugar

½ teaspoon salt

1½ teaspoons dark soy sauce

1 egg

Salt and pepper

**As one of the most expensive ingredients in Chinese cuisine, shark fin has been served at banquets and special occasions since the Song dynasty. In the 1960s, street vendors created a popular version of the traditional shark fin soup, replacing the luxury ingredient with cellophane noodles so that the less fortunate can enjoy this delicacy, too. *(Davina)***

Soak the wood ear mushrooms, shiitake mushrooms, and cellophane noodles separately in 3 bowls of hot water for 1 hour to soften. Thinly slice all the mushrooms. Cut the noodles into 1¼-inch (3-cm) lengths.

Make a slurry by mixing the cornstarch with 2 tablespoons of water.

Put the broth into a large saucepan. Add the ginger, sliced mushrooms, noodles and meat and bring to a boil. Reduce the heat to low. Add the wine, pepper, sugar, salt, and dark soy sauce. Mix well and adjust the seasoning if required. Slowly add one-third of the slurry while stirring continuously. Repeat the operation until the soup has a syrupy consistency.

Beat the egg and slowly add to the soup, swirling with a chopstick in a zigzag motion to form ribbons.

You can serve the soup immediately as is, or drizzle it with a little Akasu red vinegar.

2 P.M. / 5 P.M.

# BAGGED NOODLES

**Serves 2**
**Preparation time 10 minutes**
**Cooking time 5 minutes**

250 g fresh egg noodles
1 tablespoon sesame oil
¼ cup (40 g) canned corn kernels
½ cup (40 g) seaweed (wakame) salad
½ cup (40 g) bean sprouts, blanched
2 imitation crab sticks, shredded
Other toppings of your choice

**FOR THE SAUCE:**
2 tablespoons oyster sauce
2 teaspoons sriracha sauce
2 teaspoons light soy sauce
1 teaspoon sesame oil
2 cloves garlic, grated

**Street food in Hong Kong isn't just considered a snack but an integral part of everyday life. It has been turned into an art form to the point where dishes as simple as noodles have been reinvented so that they can be eaten on the go. Instead of using bowls, they are presented in small plastic bags that can easily be held with one hand while using bamboo skewers as chopsticks with the other.** ***(Davina)***

Cook the noodles according to the package directions. Drain and put them into a bowl. Add the sesame oil and mix well to keep them from clumping. Set aside in the refrigerator.

Mix the sauce ingredients and strain through a fine-mesh strainer (sieve) to remove the garlic.

Prepare the toppings of your choice.

Divide the noodles between 2 freezer bags. Add the toppings and sauce. Mix carefully to coat the noodles well and serve with two bamboo skewers to use as chopsticks.

# MANGO PANCAKES

**Serves 4**
**Preparation time 10 minutes**
**Resting time 30 minutes**
**Cooking time 20 minutes**

1 ripe mango

3½ tablespoons (50 ml) vegetable oil

**FOR THE BATTER:**

1½ tablespoons (20 g) unsalted butter, softened

3 eggs

⅓ cup plus 1 tablespoon (50 g) all-purpose (plain) flour

2½ tablespoons (20 g) confectioners' (icing) sugar

1 pinch salt

1 cup (250 ml) whole (full-fat) milk

¼ cup (30 g) cornstarch (cornflour)

**FOR THE CREAM:**

2 cups (500 ml) whipping cream

1 tablespoon confectioners' (icing) sugar

To make the dough, melt the butter and beat together with the eggs. Add the flour, sugar, salt, milk, and sifted cornstarch. Whisk until smooth and lump-free. Let rest for 30 minutes.

In the meantime, cut the mango flesh into large rectangles.

To make the cream, use a handheld mixer to whip the cream with the confectioners' sugar in a chilled mixing bowl. Start on low speed, then gradually increase the speed to whip the cream to stiff peaks. Set aside in the refrigerator.

Heat the oil in a nonstick skillet (frying pan) over medium heat. Add a ladle of batter to the skillet, turning to spread the batter around without the need for a spatula. Cook for 3 to 4 minutes, until bubbles appear and the top is smooth, then flip the pancake onto a plate (yes, only cooked on one side), with the well-cooked side up. Place one mango rectangle on top of the pancake. Cover with whipped cream, fold the bottom and sides of the pancake over the filling, then roll up. Repeat the process until all the ingredients are completely used.

These filled pancakes will keep for 24 hours in the refrigerator. Unfilled, the pancakes will keep for 3 days, provided they are covered in plastic wrap (clingfilm).

## VARIATIONS

You can vary the filling, and pleasure, by substituting the mango with local seasonal fruit.

# GAI PIE

## CHICKEN PIES

**Makes 12**
**Preparation time 2 hours**
**Resting time 2 hours**
**Cooking time 45 minutes**

**FOR THE DOUGH:**

¾ cup (180 g) unsalted butter, softened
½ cup (65 g) confectioners' (icing) sugar
¼ cup plus 1 tablespoon (70 ml) whole (full-fat) milk
2½ cups (310 g) all-purpose (plain) flour
¼ teaspoon salt

**FOR THE FILLING:**

14¾ ounces (420 g) boneless chicken legs
1 teaspoon Shaoxing wine
1 teaspoon light soy sauce
1 teaspoon cornstarch (cornflour)
½ teaspoon white pepper
¼ teaspoon salt
¼ teaspoon sesame oil
1½ cups (240 g) frozen diced mixed vegetables (peas, carrots, onions)
1¾ tablespoons (25 g) unsalted butter
1½ tablespoons (20 g) all-purpose (plain) flour
¼ cup (60 ml) milk
2 tablespoons (30 ml) chicken broth (stock)

**FOR THE EGG WASH:**

1 egg yolk
1 tablespoon milk

**FOR THE GLAZE:**

1 tablespoon honey

**Given the city's colonial past, it should not be a surprise that the British art of making pies has found its way into Hong Kong cuisine, but with a local twist. Instead of white mushrooms and potatoes, cooks chose to use peas and onions, ingredients that keep better in their humid climate. *(Davina)***

To make the dough, beat the butter until smooth. Incorporate the confectioners' sugar, followed by the milk. Add the flour and salt, then mix gently (not too long) with a spatula or by hand to a smooth dough.

Divide the pastry into 2 pieces, one about 1¾ ounces (50 g) heavier than the other (to make the pie crusts). Cover the dough with plastic wrap (clingfilm) and refrigerate for at least 2 hours.

To prepare the filling, cut the chicken into small chunks and mix with the Shaoxing wine, soy sauce, cornstarch, pepper, salt, and sesame oil. Let rest for 30 minutes.

In a skillet (frying pan) over medium heat, brown the chicken. Add the thawed vegetables and sauté for 1 to 2 minutes.

Melt the butter in a saucepan over medium heat. Add the flour and stir continuously for 1 to 2 minutes. Reduce the heat to low and gradually incorporate the milk and chicken broth, whisking to a thick and smooth sauce, similar to a white (béchamel) sauce. Add the chicken and vegetables, stir, and let thicken slightly. Let cool and set aside in the refrigerator.

Preheat the oven to 400°F (200°C/Gas Mark 6).

Roll out the larger pastry piece to ⅛ inch (4 mm) thick. Using a 3¼-inch (8-cm)-diameter cookie cutter, cut out 12 disks and line 2¾-inch (7-cm)-diameter mini tart pans, lightly pressing the pastry and leaving a slight margin above the rim. Prick the pastry all over with a fork and fill with the cooled chicken mixture.

Roll out the second pastry piece to about $\frac{1}{16}$ inch (3 mm) thick and cut out another 12 disks to a diameter of $3\frac{1}{4}$ inches (8 cm). Cover each pie filling with a disk and seal the edges well. Trim off the excess pastry and score a crisscross pattern on top of the pies with the tip of a knife.

Make an egg wash by beating the egg yolk with the milk and brush over the pies, then bake for 22 to 25 minutes, until golden.

Mix the honey with 1 tablespoon hot water.

Immediately after removing the pies from the oven, brush with a thin layer of the honey glaze. This will give them a glossy sheen and a hint of sweetness. Let cool before unmolding.

6 PM / 10 PM →

# 晚餐

# 炸嫩豆腐

# FRIED SILKEN TOFU

6 P.M. / 10 P.M.

**Serves 4 as predinner nibbles (or 2 for dinner)**

**Preparation time 5 minutes**
**Cooking time 10 minutes**

2 blocks extra-firm silken tofu
¾ cup (100 g) all-purpose (plain) flour
⅓ cup (50 g) cornstarch (cornflour)
1 teaspoon salt
1 teaspoon pepper
2 cups (500 ml) vegetable oil

**This tofu is salty, peppery, soft on the inside, and crispy on the outside—and the only way to eat it is hot. I can't help but order it whenever I see it on a restaurant menu, and if anyone tries to dig in first, I can become disagreeable. *(Ada)***

Handle silken tofu carefully, because it breaks up easily. Place it on several layers of paper towels (kitchen paper) and cover with several more. Place a weight on top to squeeze out the liquid, because any moisture will prevent it from becoming crispy when cooked. However, be careful: Too heavy a weight may cause the tofu to crumble.

Mix the flour, cornstarch, salt, and pepper.

Cut the tofu into small cubes and dredge in the mixture.

Heat the oil (a pinch of flour thrown into the oil should crackle), deep-fry until golden, and drain. Deep-fry the tofu a second time until golden brown and crispy. Serve the tofu piping hot.

# WET MARKETS
## *ADA*

A few years ago, I bought two soft cotton dish cloths at PMQ,[15] one of which was printed with smiling bao buns, and the other with red lampshades. Anyone who has ever been to Hong Kong will immediately recognize those plastic lampshades, because they are found by the tens of thousands in very specific places: wet markets.

Wet markets are (mostly) covered markets that are open every day and usually cover several floors. They are where you can buy fresh produce, including fish, meat, fruit and vegetables, and spices. They name wet market comes from their damp, slippery floors, which are the result of vendors regularly washing them down with buckets of water. Despite there being little local farming, wet markets are an integral part of Hong Kong culture.

15. Standing for Police Married Quarters, what was once a residence area for young married policemen has been converted into design studios, stores, and offices.

Wander around, look at the people and the stalls, and take in the smells and sounds. There is no sight in Hong Kong more livelier and exciting sight than a wet market.

If you've ever visited Hong Kong or other parts of China, or Southeast Asia, you may have noticed that butcher stalls are difficult to handle for us Westerners. They are where you will see every part of the animals hanging, waiting to be sold. What isn't necessarily pleasant to look at is, in my opinion, entirely sustainable, because every part of the animal is consumed. Poultry are sometimes sold live, then slaughtered before your very eyes. It couldn't get any fresher.

Being an archipelago in the South China Sea, Hong Kong's markets abound with fish and seafood. I can spend hours walking from stall to stall, contemplating the metal trays and their arrays of fish with gray, white, or red scales, topped with white price tags. Shrimp (prawns), crabs, and cockles, among others, are kept in large plastic tubs and sold live or slaughtered to order. Fish and seafood are more affordable than in France.

A typical custom in Hong Kong is to buy fresh produce, then head to the top floor of a restaurant, where they will cook what you just bought because you have a craving for it.

Even if you don't buy anything, you should still wander around, look at the people and the stalls, and take in the smells and sounds. There is no sight in Hong Kong livelier and more exciting than a wet market.

# SWEET-AND-SOUR PORK

**Serves 4**
**Preparation time 10 minutes**
**Marinating time 1 hour**
**Cooking time 15 minutes**

1 pound 5 ounces (600 g) pork Boston butt (collar or neck)

1 clove garlic

1¼-inch (3-cm) length fresh ginger

3 tablespoons light soy sauce

1 red bell pepper

1 yellow bell pepper

1 green bell pepper

6 slices canned pineapple rings

1 onion

2 tablespoons (15 g) cornstarch (cornflour)

1½ tablespoons (10 g) all-purpose (plain) flour

Vegetable oil

**FOR THE SWEET-AND-SOUR SAUCE:**

2 tablespoons vegetable oil

3 tablespoons ketchup

3 tablespoons apple cider vinegar

3 tablespoons packed (soft) brown sugar

1 large pinch salt

1 large pinch white pepper

1 tablespoon cornstarch (cornflour)

**I can imagine that you're now thinking to yourself: "Ketchup in the sauce? Seriously?" Yes, I'm very serious. I thought the same thing myself out loud the first time I read a recipe for sweet-and-sour pork. Before becoming the quintessential fast-food condiment, ketchup was invented in Asia. British settlers in Southeast Asia took the recipe back to the West, where it has been gradually modified until it has become the version of ketchup we all know today, popularized by the Americans.** ***(Ada)***

Cut the pork into small chunks. Peel and grate the garlic and ginger. Rub the pork with the ginger, garlic, and soy sauce. Marinate for 1 hour.

Cut the bell peppers, pineapple, and peeled onion into large dice.

In a saucepan, mix all the liquid sauce ingredients with 2 tablespoons of water, then add the brown sugar, salt and pepper and put over low heat. Add the cornstarch and stir continuously for 5 minutes to lightly thicken the sauce.

Drain the pork. Dredge each piece in cornstarch and then flour, pressing well to make sure the flour sticks.

Heat 2 tablespoons of oil in a wok and stir-fry the pork pieces over medium heat for 8 to 10 minutes, turning just a little—or not at all to avoid disturbing the coating. Set aside.

Heat the oil a little more and return the pork pieces to the wok, this time stir-frying vigorously (if possible, shaking the wok instead of moving the pieces with a spatula) for a few minutes, then add the vegetables and sauce. Stir to coat everything well and cook so the vegetables are lightly cooked but still crunchy. The pork should be crispy.

Serve and eat quickly, before the meat soaks up too much of the sauce.

# 青紅蘿蔔粟米湯

6 P.M. / 10 P.M.

# DAIKON, CARROT, AND CORN SOUP

**Serves 4**
**Preparation time 10 minutes**
**Cooking time 1 hour**

2 carrots

½ Japanese daikon (mooli) radish

1 onion

2 ears of corn, shucked and silks removed

8½ cups (2 liters) chicken broth (stock), or 1 chicken bouillon (stock) cube

1 handful goji berries

3 dried jujubes

**Given that daikon radish is packed with vitamin C, jujubes have antioxidant properties and help to reduce cholesterol levels, and goji berries are good for the liver, eyesight, and immune system, it makes sense to enjoy this soup after the winter holidays. *(Ada)***

Peel the carrots, radish, and onion. Cut the radish and carrots into large slices, the corn cobs into 4 to 5 sections, and the onion into large dice.

Combine all the ingredients in a saucepan and bring to a boil. Lower the heat, cover, and simmer for 1 hour.

Serve hot.

6 P.M. / 10 P.M.

# PORK CHOP AND RICE CASSEROLE

**Serves 2 to 3**
**Preparation time 30 minutes**
**Marinating time 30 minutes**
**Cooking time 50 minutes**

3 boneless pork chops
2 eggs
1 tablespoon all-purpose (plain) flour
½ onion
½ teaspoon minced (very finely chopped) garlic
2 tomatoes
2 cups (300 g) cooked rice
1 cup (100 g) shredded mozzarella (or Parmesan) cheese
Vegetable oil
Salt

**FOR THE MARINADE:**
1 tablespoon light soy sauce
2 teaspoons Shaoxing wine
1 teaspoon cornstarch (cornflour)
1 teaspoon sesame oil
½ teaspoon sugar

**FOR THE SAUCE:**
½ teaspoon minced (very finely chopped) garlic
2 tablespoons tomato paste (purée)
¾ cup (170 ml) chicken broth (stock)
1 tablespoon all-purpose (plain) flour
Salt and sugar

**People are often surprised by the fact that I grew up eating a lot of cheese, although I don't mean sophisticated types, such as Camembert and Brie. Mozzarella was a regular treat, not only on pizza but in many traditional *cha chaan teng*, with baked pork chop rice being my favorite. *(Davina)***

Tenderize the pork chops using the back of a knife or a mallet. Mix the marinade ingredients, then add the chops, coat the chops well, and let marinate for about 30 minutes.

Beat the eggs. Dip the chops in the egg and dredge in the flour.

Heat a little oil in a skillet (frying pan) over medium heat and sear the chops on both sides until browned. Set aside.

Heat a little more oil and sauté the chopped onion until fragrant. Add the garlic and sauté quickly. Stir in the coarsely diced tomatoes, season with salt, and cook until soft. Set aside.

Heat a little more oil in the skillet and add the remaining beaten eggs. When they start to set, add the rice and stir-fry until well coated with egg. Stir in two-thirds of the tomatoes, then transfer to an ovenproof dish.

Preheat the oven to 425°F (220°C/Gas Mark 7).

To make the sauce, heat a little more oil and sauté the garlic. Reduce the heat to low, add the tomato paste, and mix well. Incorporate the broth and bring to a boil. Gradually add the flour, stirring continuously until the sauce thickens. Season with salt and sugar.

Add the chops and remaining tomatoes to the sauce, mix well, and then arrange the pork and sauce over the rice. Cover with the cheese and bake for 15 to 20 minutes, until golden brown.

Serve hot.

# NG TUNG CHAI

## *ADA*

When I was a French schoolgirl and about nine years old, my best friend and I invented a game we called "Little Girls of the Jungle." Our school playground became a rainforest. Before our childish eyes appeared lush greenery, waterfalls, and gigantic tree trunks that we could slide down, and we ran around imagining ourselves traversing this luxuriant landscape. However, when I hiked the Ng Tung Chai Waterfall trail, at the age of 30, I was amazed to discover that the imaginary landscapes of my childhood were actually real.

Because this trail is in the middle of the New Territories, it requires a great deal of effort. It takes more than an hour by Metro, bus, and sometimes even a taxicab to get to the starting point, where you are greeted by a sign advising you to be physically and psychologically strong enough to do the hike. It is also recommended that you wear long clothing and apply mosquito repellent. The first time I attempted this hike, I didn't meet all the requirements. It also started raining so hard that I lost a contact lens. I only made it to the first waterfall before giving up. When the weather improved, and now slathered in mosquito repellent, wearing long pants, and being psychologically and physically prepared, I went back to try again.

As in my childhood games, I clambered over the thick intertwining roots on the forest floor and mountainside, hung from tree branches (confirming that they too were solid), and admired every shade of green and shape of the leaves. More than anything, I marveled at the waterfalls.

When I reached the first waterfall, I took a cautious dip in the clear water of its pool, being careful to avoid slipping on the sticky pebbles, and I was immediately refreshed. I had the waterfall to myself for half an hour before another hiker stopped by.

I then climbed up to the second waterfall, which was not far away. Despite wanting to bathe again, I just jumped from stone to stone, listening to the sound of the falling water, whose roar I tend to find as unsettling as it is soothing.

The third waterfall, which can be reached after a 15-minute climb, was more open. Sunlight might even reach it directly sometimes. I lay down on a large, cold rock and spent a few minutes just listening to the sounds of the forest. I made out the creaking of branches, water trickling from everywhere, not just the waterfall, as well as the wind and the sounds coming from the mountain.

The fourth waterfall was the most impressive of all. Its seemed to fall straight from the sky and in a thinner stream, as if it were salt rather than water. I washed my face in it (it would have been a shame to leave the forest without cleansing my soul) and carried on. Although I had finished with the waterfalls, there was still another pool and I couldn't resist another dip. A magnificent view over the entire valley could be seen through an opening between the tree branches. I managed a couple of strokes in the pool and then got dressed. It was so easy to lose track of time, and I still had to make my way home.

As in my childhood games, I clambered over the thick intertwining roots on the forest floor and mountainside, hung from tree branches, and admired every shade of green and shape of the leaves. More than anything, I marveled at the waterfalls.

# 焗肉醬意粉

# SPAGHETTI BOLOGNESE CASSEROLE

**Serves 4**
**Preparation time 20 minutes**
**Marinating time 1 hour**
**Cooking time 1 hour 15 minutes**

7 ounces (200 g) ground (minced) beef
2 tablespoons cornstarch (cornflour)
3 tablespoons light soy sauce
2½ tablespoons (30 g) sugar
2 cloves garlic
1 onion
1 carrot
2 tomatoes
4 sprigs thyme
1 sprig rosemary
2 tablespoons ketchup
2 tablespoons tomato paste (purée)
2 cups (500 ml) tomato puree (passata)
11¼ ounces (320 g) spaghetti
1⅓ cups (150 g) shredded mozzarella cheese
Olive oil
Salt and pepper

**This baked spaghetti Bolognese is the Hong Kong version of lasagna. Like most tomato-based dishes, it has a sweeter taste that the one we are accustomed to in Europe. *(Ada)***

Mix together the ground meat, cornstarch, soy sauce, and sugar. Refrigerate for 1 hour.

Peel, chop, and finely dice the garlic, onion, and carrot. Finely dice the tomatoes.

Heat 1 tablespoon of oil in a skillet (frying pan), then reduce the heat to low and sauté the thyme, rosemary, and onion with the garlic and carrots for 10 to 15 minutes, until they brown and the onions start to soften. Add the meat and crumble with a wooden spoon. When the meat starts to color, incorporate the tomatoes, ketchup, and tomato paste, then deglaze with scant 1 cup (200 ml) of water. Mix well. Add the tomato puree and season with salt and pepper. Cover with a lid and simmer for 45 minutes over low heat.

Cook the pasta according to the package directions. Drain and mix with the sauce.

Preheat the oven to 350°F (180°C/Gas Mark 4).

Transfer the spaghetti Bolognese to an ovenproof dish, cover with the cheese, and bake for about 15 minutes, until the cheese melts and turns golden brown.

6 P.M. / 10 P.M.

# HONG KONG-STYLE BORSCH

**Serves 4**
**Preparation** time **30 minutes**
**Cooking time 2 hours 15 minutes**

4 tomatoes
½ green cabbage
4 celery stalks
2 potatoes
2 carrots
1 red onion
2 cloves garlic
2-inch (5-cm) length ginger
1 pound 2 ounces (500 g) oxtail
1 teaspoon salt
1 tablespoon vegetable oil
¼ cup (70 g) ketchup
2 cups (500 ml) chicken broth (stock)
½ lemon
1 bay leaf
Sugar
Salt and pepper

**Did you think borsch was a beet (beetroot) soup from Eastern Europe? So did I. And this is true. But it's also an extremely popular soup in Hong Kong—in fact, it has become an iconic dish in the local cuisine and is often featured as an appetizer on the set menus of soy sauce Western restaurants (see page 48). Why is this so, and how did this soup end up in Hong Kong? To understand this, we need to go back to 1917. In the wake of the Russian Revolution, many Russians who supported the czar and were against the communists fled to Vladivostok, Russia's easternmost city, which is close to the border with North Korea. As communist rule was consolidated in the 1920s and 1930s, the political situation became critical, and many Russians were forced to take refuge in China, or more precisely in Shanghai. At the time, it had an open port and did not require visas or permits to stay there. The Russians easily found work in the restaurant business, where they served a version of their borsch adapted to local ingredients. Because beets could not be found in Shanghai, they were substituted with cabbage and tomatoes. The Chinese Communist Revolution of 1949 forced the Russian emigrés into exile once again, and this time they chose Hong Kong, then under British rule. And that is how borsch came to settle in Hong Kong, after a journey that took more than 30 years. *(Ada)***

Cut 3 tomatoes into large dice and finely dice the last one.

Remove the cabbage core and cut the leaves lengthwise into thick strips.

Trim the bottom of the celery and break the stalks in half by hand to make the strings appear. Destring and coarsely chop the stalks.

Peel and cut the potatoes and carrots into large chunks.

Peel and coarsely chop the onion.

Peel the garlic and ginger and crush both with the blade of a knife.

Put the oxtail into a saucepan, then add the salt and 6⅓ cups (1.5 liters) of cold water. Bring to a boil, then turn down the heat and simmer for 1 minute. Submerge the meat in ice cold water to remove any impurities.

Heat the oil in a wok (or use a casserole or cooking pot) over medium heat and sauté the onion, garlic, and ginger for a few minutes. When they begin to color, add the tomatoes. Sauté for 1 minute, then add the potatoes and carrots. Increase the heat to brown the contents of the wok, then add the celery, followed by the ketchup. Mix well, and finally add the beef.

If you've browned your vegetables in a wok, transfer them now to a casserole or cooking pot.

Add the chicken broth and 4¼ cups (1 liter) of water, along with the lemon half, cabbage, and bay leaf. Mix well. Cover with a lid and bring to a boil, then reduce the heat to medium and simmer for 2 hours.

Taste and adjust the seasoning. This soup should be a little sweet, unlike the sour Eastern European version. You can add 1 to 2 tablespoons of sugar, 1 pinch of salt, and/or 1 pinch of pepper.

# FISH-FRAGRANT EGGPLANT

**Serves 4**
**Preparation time 15 minutes**
**Cooking time 10 minutes**

3 cloves garlic
1¼-inch (3-cm) length fresh ginger
3 scallions (spring onions)
5 Chinese eggplants (aubergines)
3½ ounces (100 g) ground (minced) pork
1 red chile
Vegetable oil

**FOR THE SAUCE:**
2 tablespoons light soy sauce
2 tablespoons oyster sauce
2 tablespoons black rice vinegar
1 tablespoon dark soy sauce
1 tablespoon packed (soft) brown sugar
1 tablespoon sesame oil
1 tablespoon cornstarch (cornflour)

**Although this recipe originated in Sichuan, a region in central China, it is widely eaten in Hong Kong. Despite its name, it doesn't contain fish, although some recipes add 1 tablespoon XO sauce (see page 186) for a flavor that is even more reminiscent of the sea. *(Ada)***

Mix all the sauce ingredients in a bowl with 2 tablespoons of water.

Peel and chop the garlic and ginger. Slice the scallions, separating the white bulb from the green leaves. Cut the eggplants in half lengthwise, then into large chunks.

Steam the eggplants for 5 minutes.

Heat 1 tablespoon oil in a wok, add the garlic and ginger, then the ground meat and 1 tablespoon of the sauce, and crumble the meat with a wooden spoon. Let brown for a few minutes. Add the sliced scallion bulbs, eggplant, and the remaining sauce, then increase the heat to high. Stir briskly for 2 to 3 minutes to thoroughly sear the ingredients.

Serve hot, sprinkled with chopped chile and the scallion leaves.

## VARIATIONS

You can substitute the pork with ground (minced) beef.

For the vegetarian version, omit the ground meat and replace the oyster sauce with tamari.

# STEAMED FISH

**Serves 4 (or serve with other dishes for a celebratory banquet)**

**Preparation time 10 minutes**

**Cooking time 20 minutes**

2-inch (5-cm) length fresh ginger

3 scallions (spring onions)

1 sea bass (about 1½ pounds/700 g) cleaned and prepared by your fish dealer

¼ cup (60 ml) light soy sauce

1 tablespoon sugar

½ bunch fresh cilantro (coriander)

Vegetable oil

**This is probably my favorite dish. I love the ultratender fish that you gently loosen with a chopstick to dip into the sauce, as well as the little kick from the scallions and coriander, the saltiness of the soy sauce, and the roundness of the ginger-flavored oil. I love having it with Davina when we get together shortly after the Lunar New Year. *(Ada)***

Peel and cut the ginger into thin matchsticks. Separate the scallions into white bulbs and green leaves, then thinly slice them. Rinse the fish to make sure that all the scales have been removed.

Arrange the fish on a dish, sprinkle with the ginger inside and out, and steam for 10 to 15 minutes, depending on its size. It is cooked when you prick the flesh with a chopstick and it comes out dry. Drain any excess water after cooking.

To steam the fish, use a large steamer that can fit a casserole; alternatively, place the fish on a plate, pour scant 1 cup (200 ml) water into the bottom of a pot, put a metal mixing bowl upside down inside the pot, and place the plate on top of the bowl.

Sprinkle the scallions over the fish.

Heat 4 large tablespoons of oil until very hot. Be careful when doing this, because the oil will catch fire if the temperature is too hot. You must watch it closely. As soon as the oil begins to smoke, pour it over the fish and scallions.

Heat the soy sauce and sugar with 2 tablespoons of water. Pour the sauce around the fish, but not directly over it, to prevent the flesh from becoming spongy. Sprinkle with the cilantro and serve.

## TIP

Don't forget to try the cheek—it's the tenderest part of the fish.

6 P.M. / 10 P.M.

# 椒鹽鮮魷

# SALT-AND-PEPPER SQUID

**Serves 4**
**Preparation time 10 minutes**
**Cooking time 3 minutes**

8¾ ounces (250 g) small squid
1 tablespoon Sichuan peppercorns
1 tablespoon black peppercorns
1 teaspoon salt
¾ cup (100 g) cornstarch (cornflour)
2 cloves garlic
2 scallions (spring onions)
2 cups (500 ml) vegetable oil
1 egg
1 teaspoon chili powder (optional)

**I first came across this dish at a Chinese restaurant in Paris, without knowing that it was a specialty of Hong Kong. I'm obsessed with the combination of the salt and pepper, the crunchy texture, and the comforting warmth of these little pieces of squid that make great predinner nibbles. Over time, I have come to realize that this dish features on the menu of many *dai pa dongs* in Hong Kong, which is not surprising, given the abundance of seafood. *(Ada)***

Cut the squid into thick strips.

Toast the peppercorns in a dry skillet (frying pan), then grind in a mortar (or in a blender, if you're feeling lazy). Mix with the salt and cornstarch.

Chop the garlic and white scallion bulbs. Bring 3½ tablespoons (50 ml) of oil to a boil, then pour it over the garlic and scallions.

Heat the remaining oil in a saucepan or deep fryer.

Dredge the squid in the salt and pepper mixture, then dip it in beaten egg. When the oil is hot, deep-fry the squid for 2 to 3 minutes, then drain well. Add the garlic and chopped scallion bulbs to the squid.

Chop the scallion leaves and sprinkle them over the squid. Add a touch of chili powder, if using. Serve hot.

## NOTE

There are also versions of this recipe for cuttlefish and larger squid. I'll leave it up to you to work out the difference between cuttlefish, squid, and octopus.

There are tons of different recipes: some suggest dredging the squid only in cornstarch; others call for breadcrumbs, either plain or panko; while others include the batter used for fish and chips. After testing all of these versions (and having the delicious smell waft through my apartment for several days) I settled on this one. But you can have fun trying them all out, too.

# SAI KUNG
## *ADA*

About ten years ago, my father went to Hong Kong for work reasons. He called me, and I remember well what he said: "Hong Kong is crazy! But on the flip side, there's nothing to do here. Four days is more than enough to see everything."

Unlike him, I was lucky to discover this place through contacts I made with people who had lived there for years, who could show me all of its hidden gems. One of those places I could have never found on my own is Sai Kung.

It was a real trek from Hong Kong Island by subway, bus, minibus, etc. But at the end was a quiet harbor and a fishing village, where the sky seemed nearer and where you could hear seagulls. There were no speedboats running that day to reach the start of the legendary 60-mile (100-km)-long MacLehose Trail, because the sea was too choppy. Instead, I took a taxicab to the Pavilion. The driver warned me that there was no cell phone signal there, so he gave me some numbers to call as soon as the signal came back, otherwise it would be a nightmare for me to get home.

The birds, the wind, and the butterflies. I felt like a princess from an animated movie as I gazed at the turquoise sea from between the bushes.

I started the trail with gusto. I had no earphones, just the birds, the wind, and the butterflies. I felt like a princess from an animated movie (wearing shorts and sneakers) as I gazed at the turquoise sea from between the bushes. I passed a buffalo, which seemed unperturbed by my presence. The sun was beating down, and I began to sweat.

After a downhill stretch, I walked along the river. I decided to defy a prohibition sign and make my way to the Four Consecutive Rock Pools. The place was deserted, the water cool and clear. I soak my legs, alone in the world—until I was encroached upon by a group of noisy children.

I resumed my walk and came to a long and beautiful beach, like one you might see in a commercial. The water was blue and the sand was white, but there were dangerous currents. As I waded in the sea, I felt hungry. My phone battery was now dead—I'd taken too many photos. I welcomed the sight of a small empty restaurant. For 10 Hong Kong dollars, I was able to recharge my phone (and my strength with a ginger egg fried rice).

As I was about to leave, a man shouted: "Speedboat!" There would be one leaving in an hour's time. I sat on the sand and waited, ice cream in hand and the November sun on my face.

When the boat arrived, I boarded barefoot, salt stinging my blisters. I sat at the front of the speedboat, with my glasses put away and the wind and spray whipping my face. I watched the islands go by, and the red cliffs, trees, foam. I closed my eyes. It was a vacation day within a vacation.

Back at the harbor, life went on: schoolchildren, families, helpers laden with shopping. I was faced by another ride on a double-decker bus, more subway trains, and then a minibus to get back home.

# XO SAUCE

**For 1 jar (about 1 pound/500 g)**
**Preparation time 30 minutes**
**Soaking time 2 hours**
**Cooking time 1 hour**

5¼ ounces (150 g) dried scallops
4¼ ounces (120 g) dried shrimp
2½ ounces (75 g) Jinhua ham
6 cloves (20 g) garlic
4 (75 g) shallots
4 fresh chiles (or as desired, according to preference)
½ cup (20 g) dried chiles (or as desired, according to preference)
1¾ cups (400 ml) vegetable oil
2 tablespoons sugar
1 tablespoon light soy sauce
2 tablespoons abalone sauce
1 tablespoon oyster sauce
2 tablespoons Shaoxing wine

**XO sauce, one of Hong Kong's most emblematic condiments, is prized in both home and professional kitchens around the world. Rich in umami and containing prestigious ingredients, such as dried scallops and Jinhua ham, it enhances even the simplest dishes with its intense flavor, rich texture, and hint of heat. *(Davina)***

Soak the dried scallops and shrimp separately in 2 bowls of boiling water for 2 hours. Cut the ham into cubes. Peel and finely chop the garlic and shallots, ideally using a food processor. Chop the fresh and dried chiles into small pieces, then remove the seeds using a strainer (sieve).

Drain the scallops and shrimp. Place the scallops and ham in a heatproof bowl, steam for 15 minutes, and let cool. Shred the scallops in a food processor to short threads. Coarsely chop the shrimp in a food processor.

Heat the oil in a pot or deep skillet to 400°F (200°C) over medium-low heat. Fry the shallots, garlic, and chiles until golden. Strain the flavored oil and reuse to fry the shrimp over medium-low heat until brown. Remove them from the oil and set aside. Repeat the process with the ham and scallops.

Remove them from the heat and stir the sugar into the still-hot oil until completely dissolved. Add the soy sauce, abalone sauce, Shaoxing wine, and oyster sauce, then place over low heat and stir briefly. Add the fried ingredients and mix carefully to combine, then transfer the sauce to a jar and let cool to room temperature before sealing.

This sauce can be used for many dishes, including stir-fries, noodles, and steamed rice.

6 P.M. / 10 P.M.

# BO ZAI FAN

## CLAY POT RICE

**Serves 2**
**Preparation time 20 minutes**
**Soaking time 30 minutes**
**Cooking time 35 minutes**
**Resting time 5 minutes**

1⅔ cups (300 g) jasmine (Thai fragrant) rice

2 Chinese sausages (*lap cheong*) or 1 *lap cheong* plus 1 liver sausage

4 Chinese broccoli (*kai lan*) stems (stalks) with leaves

1 egg yolk

Chives

Vegetable oil

**FOR THE SAUCE:**

1 tablespoon vegetable oil

1 scallion (spring onion)

2 cloves garlic

1½ tablespoons (10 g) minced (very finely chopped) fresh ginger

1 tablespoon Shaoxing wine

3 tablespoons light soy sauce

3 tablespoons dark soy sauce

2 tablespoons sugar

**Winter smells different in every corner of the world. In France, it's the rich aroma of raclette cheese mixed with the smoke of an open fire. In Japan, the air is filled with the aroma of the roasted sweet potatoes sold by street vendors. In Hong Kong, nothing heralds the arrival of winter like the irresistible smell of clay pot rice as it crackles on the flame, the soy sauce caramelizing at the bottom of the pot, and the smoking sausage. *(Davina)***

Rinse the rice carefully and soak it in 1¼ cups (300 ml) of cold water for 30 minutes.

To make the sauce, heat the oil in a small saucepan over medium heat and sauté the scallions, cut into 1½-inch (4-cm) lengths, with the crushed garlic and minced ginger for about 2 minutes, until they release their aroma and turn golden. Add the Shaoxing wine, 5 teaspoons (25 ml) of hot water, the light soy sauce, dark soy sauce, and sugar. Bring to a boil over high heat, then reduce the heat and simmer for about 8 minutes, until the sauce thickens slightly. Strain through a fine-mesh strainer (sieve).

Bring a saucepan of water to a boil to blanch the sausages for 3 minutes, which will remove any excess fat and impurities. Use the same water to blanch the Chinese broccoli for 1 to 2 minutes, then drain.

Lightly grease the bottom of a 6¼ to 7-inch (16 to 18-cm)-diameter clay pot with oil. Add the rice along with its soaking water and bring to a boil over high heat. Reduce the heat to medium-low, cover with a lid, and cook for 5 minutes.

Remove the lid and place the sausages over the rice, then cover again and cook for another 15 minutes over medium-low heat, turning the pot a little every 2 to 3 minutes to be sure of even cooking.

When the rice is cooked, thinly slice the sausages on the diagonal and arrange the slices on the rice. Add the Chinese broccoli and turn off the heat. Cover the pot and let stand for 5 minutes so the flavors can blend. Garnish with chopped chives, top with egg yolk, drizzle generously with sauce, and serve immediately. The scorched, or crispy, layer of rice at the bottom of the pot is the most prized part of this dish.

6 P.M. / 10 P.M.

# 避風塘炒蟹

# TYPHOON SHELTER FRIED CRAB

**Serves 2 to 3**
**Preparation time 15 minutes**
**Soaking time 30 minutes**
**Freezing time 15 minutes**
**Cooking time 20 minutes**

- 1 live crab (preferably a mud crab, but other local varieties are suitable)
- 8 garlic bulbs
- 3 cups (700 ml) vegetable oil
- 2 tablespoons fermented soybeans
- 2 Thai (bird's eye) chiles
- 4 scallions (spring onions)
- 2 tablespoons minced (very finely chopped) garlic
- ½ teaspoon crushed red pepper (chili) flakes (or as desired, according to preference)
- Light soy sauce
- Salt

**While many of the signature Hong Kong dishes are inspired by other cultures, typhoon shelter fried crab is a purely local creation created by the fishing community. Although this dish can be found in many Hong Kong restaurants today, the best can still be found in the restaurants located around the Causeway Bay typhoon shelter, where it all began. *(Davina)***

Soak the crab in a large bowl of water with 1 tablespoon of salt for 30 minutes to expel impurities. Rinse the crab and place it in the freezer for 15 minutes to numb.

Peel and mince (very finely chop) the garlic bulbs in a food processor.

Heat the oil in a small saucepan over medium-low heat. Add the minced garlic and fry until lightly colored. Drain, collecting the oil, and set both aside.

Remove the crab from the freezer. Using a sharp knife, cut out the abdominal flap on the underside of the crab and discard. Turn the crab over and lift off the shell in one piece. Using kitchen shears, remove the beak, gills, and pointed ends of the legs. Next, cut the crab in half, first widthwise and then lengthwise. Use a mallet to gently crack the cavities so that the spices can better penetrate the flesh when cooked.

Heat the garlic-flavored oil in a large wok over high heat. When the oil temperature reaches 350°F (180°C), add the crab meat, followed by the shell about 1minute later. Fry the meat for 3 minutes, until golden, then drain. Set aside 3 tablespoons of the frying oil and discard the rest.

Finely chop the fermented soybeans. Dice the chiles and remove the seeds. Cut the scallions into 1½-inch (4-cm) lengths.

Heat the 3 tablespoons of previously reserved oil in the wok and sauté the soybeans, minced garlic, scallions, and chiles over medium-high heat until all the ingredients release their aroma. Add the crab, previously fried garlic, and red pepper flakes and mix well. Season with salt and soy sauce, plate on a serving dish, and serve immediately.

# BEEF BRISKET CURRY

**Serves 2 to 3**
**Preparation time 40 minutes**
**Cooking time 2 hours 30 minutes to 3 hours**

1 pound 2 ounces (500 g) beef brisket
4 slices ginger
2 scallions (spring onions)
1 tablespoon chu hou paste
2 tablespoons Shaoxing wine
4 bay leaves
2 star anise
½ ounce (15 g) Chinese rock sugar (available in Chinese grocery stores) or sugar lumps (or 1½ tablespoons/15 g granulated sugar)
1 to 2 carrots
3 medium (300 g) potatoes
3 cloves garlic
1 onion
1 tablespoon curry paste
2 teaspoons curry powder
¼ cup (60 ml) unsweetened coconut cream
1 tablespoon evaporated milk
Vegetable oil
Salt and pepper

**Curries have always fascinated me. They can be found in many countries, and each has its own distinctive touch. Hong Kong-style curry contains less spice than Indian curries—curry powder is used instead of whole spices— and are almost always made with unsweetened coconut milk or cream, often accompanied by beef brisket and served with a bowl of rice. *(Davina)***

Rinse the brisket and cut into 1½ to 2-inch (4 to 5-cm) pieces. Place the meat in a pot with 2 ginger slices and cover the contents of the pot with water. Place over high heat and bring to a boil. Cover and cook for 3 minutes. Drain the beef and rinse in cold water.

Cut the scallions into 1½ to 2-inch (4 to 5-cm) lengths.

In a pot, heat 2 tablespoons of oil over medium-high heat and sauté the remaining ginger slices and the scallions until they release their aroma. Add the chu hou paste and Shaoxing wine, then mix well. Add the meat and cook for 5 minutes. Cover again with water (2 cups/500 ml). Add 2 of the bay leaves, the star anise, and sugar. Bring to a boil over medium-high heat, then cover and simmer over low heat for 1 hour.

In the meantime, cut the carrots and potatoes into 1¼-inch (3-cm) chunks.

After 1 hour, remove the meat from the pot and set aside the cooking liquid. Heat 1 tablespoon of oil in a saucepan over medium heat and sauté the carrots and potatoes until lightly colored. Set aside.

Chop the garlic and onion. Add another 1 tablespoon oil to the pan and sauté them over medium heat until fragrant. Add the curry paste and curry powder and stir to incorporate.

Add the brisket, stir, then incorporate the cooking liquid with the remaining bay leaves. Bring to a boil over high heat, then reduce the heat to low and simmer for 30 minutes. Add the carrots and potatoes and simmer for another 30 minutes.

Finally, add the coconut cream and evaporated milk. Adjust the seasoning with salt and pepper and let simmer for another 10 minutes. Serve hot accompanied with a bowl of rice or a baguette.

# 薑汁豆腐花

6 P.M. / 10 P.M.

# SILKEN TOFU PUDDING WITH GINGER SYRUP

**Serves 2**
**Preparation time 5 minutes**
**Cooking time 20 minutes**

2-inch (5-cm) length ginger

1 ounce (25 g) Chinese yellow rock sugar (available in Chinese grocery stores) or sugar lumps (or 2 tablespoons/25 g granulated sugar)

2 tablespoons (25 g) packed soft brown sugar

7 ounces (200 g) silken tofu, chilled

Slice the ginger. In a saucepan, combine the sugars and ginger with 2 cups (500 ml) of water and bring to a boil.

Let the syrup simmer for about 20 minutes.

Divide the tofu into two bowls and pour over the hot ginger syrup.

## NOTE

Feel free to adjust the amount of ginger to suit your taste.

# RED BEAN SOUP

**Serves 6**
**Preparation time 30 minutes**
**Soaking time 12 hours plus 30 minutes**
**Cooking time 2 hours**

¾ cup (150 g) red (adzuki) beans

1 small (1 g) dried tangerine peel or 1 teaspoon freshly grated orange zest

2 ounces (60 g) Chinese rock sugar (available in Chinese grocery stores) or sugar lumps (or ⅓ cup/60 g granulated sugar)

Coconut milk (optional)

Lily bulbs, lotus seeds, tapioca pearls, etc. (optional, for added texture)

**There is a category of desserts in Hong Kong known as *tong sui* (糖水), and its literal translation is "sweet water." However, the apparent simplicity of the term is deceptive. Ranging from modest dishes, such as red bean soup, to more refined creations, such as bird's nest soup, *tong sui*, or dessert soups, pay homage to the city's Cantonese heritage by transforming simple ingredients, such as sugar, water, grains, and beans, into a wide variety of sweet delicacies. *(Davina)***

Cover the beans in plenty of water and soak for 12 hours overnight.

On the actual day, soak the dried tangerine peel in water for 30 minutes to rehydrate. Gently scrape off the pith skin and cut in half.

In a saucepan, bring 6⅓ cups (1.5 liters) water to a boil. Add the beans and tangerine peel, cover, and reduce the heat to medium. Simmer for 1 hour 30 minutes, stirring regularly to keep the beans from sticking to the bottom. Add more water if necessary.

If you prefer a grainier texture, gently mash the beans. Add the sugar and stir until completely dissolved. Simmer for another 25 minutes.

This soup can be served hot or cold. If you like, add coconut milk and lily bulbs before serving.

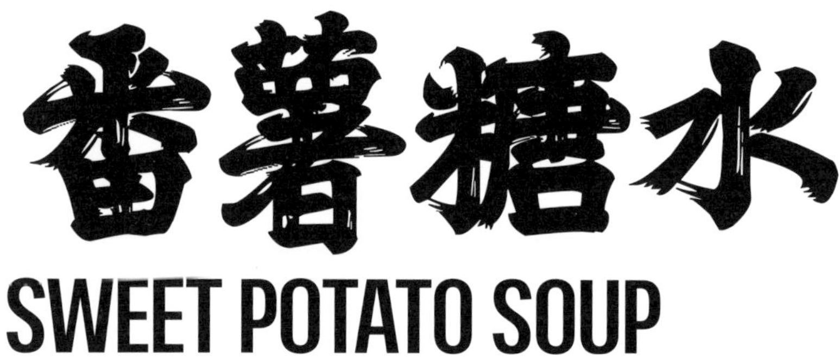


6 P.M. / 10 P.M.

# SWEET POTATO SOUP

**Serves 2**
**Preparation time 10 minutes**
**Cooking time 30 minutes**

1¾ ounces (50 g) fresh ginger (about ½ cup prepared)

3 medium (400 g) sweet potatoes

2⅛ ounces (60 g) slab sugar (or ⅓ cup/60 g packed soft brown sugar)

**If you're wondering what I turn to when I want to warm up on cold winter days, it isn't hot chocolate or raclette cheese, but a steaming bowl of sweet potato soup. This is a comforting treat my mother often made in winter. *(Davina)***

Peel and thinly slice the ginger. Lightly crush it with the flat of a knife to release its aromas. Peel the sweet potatoes, cut them into medium chunks, and soak in water to keep them from oxidizing. Be careful not to cut the pieces too small, or they may soften too much when cooked.

Bring 4¼ cups (1 liter) of water to a simmer in a saucepan, add the ginger, and cook for 10 minutes over medium heat. Add the sweet potatoes and sugar, cover, and cook for another 15 to 20 minutes.

Turn off the heat and uncover to stop the sweet potatoes from continuing to cook in the residual steam. Serve piping hot for a moment of winter warmth.

6 P.M. / 10 P.M.

# MANGO PUDDING

**Serves 2 to 3**
**Preparation time 15 minutes**
**Refrigeration time 4 hours**

3 sheets (leaves) gelatin
2 ripe mangoes
1 cup (250 ml) evaporated milk

**This dessert is from the British colonial period and was invented after the introduction of gelatin and agar-agar to Hong Kong. Local chefs were inspired to incorporate these new products into recipes using local ingredients, such as fresh mango. Although there are variations of this dessert with coconut milk, I prefer this simpler version. I love its creamy texture and its bursting fragrance of ripe mango. *(Ada)***

Soak the gelatin sheets in a glass of cold water until softened.

Peel one and a half the mangoes and cut them into pieces. Blend to a smooth puree.

In a saucepan, heat ⅔ cup (150 ml) of the evaporated milk over low heat. Squeeze the gelatin, dissolve in the milk, and incorporate the mango puree.

Fill molds or bowls and refrigerate for at least 4 hours.

Immediately before serving, dice the remaining mango half. Drizzle the remaining evaporated milk over the puddings, add the diced mango, and serve chilled.

# INDEX BY INGREDIENT

## P



## R



## S

## T



## V



## W



## Y

## CONTRIBUTORS

Felix Cheung, also known as FatCheFelix, is a renowned private chef based in Hong Kong with a talent for marrying traditional culinary techniques with local influences. He has been profoundly influenced by the culinary cultures of Hong Kong and Taiwan, where he was raised. After career-defining experiences at prestigious restaurants in Melbourne, New York, and London, he has returned to Hong Kong, where he delights customers with dishes inspired by his roots and international adventures.

Eloise, a dedicated member of the Bing Sutt team, is originally from Hong Kong and has lived in Paris for more than ten years. Her passion for cooking has driven her to reproduce the authentic flavors of her homeland and introduce them to as many people as possible, starting with her daughter. In the past, Eloise has hosted a YouTube channel on which she shared her mother's recipes. Her goal is to help fellow expats everywhere to rediscover the comforting flavors of home.

## ACKNOWLEDGMENTS

Many thanks to Julie and Julien, without whom my love affair with Hong Kong would not exist. Thank you for your support, your hospitality, your presence, and your advice; in short, thank you for everything. Thank you Owen and Leny for lending me your rooms and beds, and to Zoé for accompanying me on my expedition to Peng Chau and Cheung Chau. This book is for all five of you.

A huge thank you too, Davina, for welcoming me, my intensity, and my ambitious projects into your life. Thank you for opening Bing Sutt; thank you for making the best pineapple buns I've ever eaten (and we know I've eaten a few); thank you for your beautiful photographs, your talent, your humor, and your patience. It was an infinite pleasure to work with you on this project.

Thanks to Marjorie and Fanny for supporting our project. Thank you for your kindness, your presence, your advice, your attentiveness, and for following us. We are lucky to have the support we need to accomplish something that has been so close to our hearts. Many thanks to Marie for her meticulous proofreading.

Thank you Lucas for helping me to discover remote and unknown corners of Hong Kong; thank you for everything you taught me about Hong Kong, China, history, and architecture; thank you for your camera, of course; and thank you for your advice and for all the time you took to take me on photography shoots, even late on weeknights in Kowloon.

A huge thank you to Sarah for your sponsorship, which enabled me to finish my reports.

Thanks to Paulus for putting up with my stopping every 30 seconds to take photos, although I passed the same spot every day and would have weeks to do so.

Thanks to all the people I met in Hong Kong, for feeding me with anecdotes, stories, recommendations for restaurants and dishes to try, and for your support.

Thank you to all my friends, family, and acquaintances who have listened to me talk about Hong Kong for more than two years. I'm not done yet.

Ada

I would like to express my sincere gratitude to my family for passing on to me the culture and traditions of Hong Kong, and for filling my childhood with the authentic flavors of Cantonese cuisine. A big thank you to my mom, who made sure that although I went to an international school, I never forgot the traditions and language that have shaped me into the person I am today.

A huge thank you to Ada, who came in one morning looking for a pineapple bun and a cup of milk tea. Without you, this book would not exist. As I mentioned in the introduction, you're one of the reasons I appreciate my Hong Kong roots even more, and I feel honored to be able to represent them in such a meaningful way here in Paris. Thank you for trusting me to cowrite this book with you, for allowing me to be part of one of your greatest passions, and for helping me to rediscover my city as we explored every corner of it during our photo shoots.

Thanks to Nico, my boyfriend, for your support throughout this project. Your enthusiasm for sampling (and finishing off) the recipes that Ada and I tested in Paris has touched me enormously. I am eternally grateful to have found someone so eager to discover my culture and understand what makes me who I am.

To all my friends, thank you for being there throughout this project and my life. Thank you for your patience and understanding, especially during the days when I decided to cancel my plans to concentrate on writing. A special thanks to my Hong Kong friends in Paris, who remind me of my roots with our Cantonese jokes and Hong Kong pop culture gossip, despite the 5,975 miles (9,620 km) that separate us from home.

Thank you, Fanny and Marjorie, for entrusting us with this project, for your advice in the making of this book, and, above all, for helping me to realize a childhood dream: to write a book.

And finally, thanks to all my Bing Sutt customers, especially those who have lived in or visited Hong Kong. Every day at the café, I hear different anecdotes that remind me of little pieces of life in Hong Kong, reminding me that this incredible city is really part of me.

Davina

Originally published in 2025 by Solar, an imprint of Édi 8, under the title *Hong Kong à la carte. Une Journée dans les cuisines Hong Kongaises.*


For the English edition:

A member of Penguin Random House Verlagsgruppe GmbH
Neumarkter Strasse 28 · 81673 Munich

1st edition 2026

produktsicherheit@penguinrandomhouse.de
(The above information is mandatory information according to GPSR and should be used for all queries relating to the safety of our books)



A CIP catalogue record for this book is available from the British Library.

Editorial direction Prestel: Claudia Schönecker
Project management: Veronika Brandt
Translation: John Ripoll and Theresa Bebbington
for Cillero & de Motta
Copyediting and typesetting: Cillero & de Motta, booklab GmbH
Cover design: Studio Mahr
Production management: Luisa Klose
Printing and binding: Pollina, France

Printed in France

ISBN 978-3-7913-9185-4

www.prestel.com